Florence E Burch

Dick and Harry and Tom

Or, for our reaping by-and-by

Florence E Burch

Dick and Harry and Tom
Or, for our reaping by-and-by

ISBN/EAN: 9783337106140

Printed in Europe, USA, Canada, Australia, Japan

Cover: Foto ©ninafisch / pixelio.de

More available books at **www.hansebooks.com**

DICK AND HARRY AND TOM

OR

"𝔉𝔬𝔯 𝔒𝔲𝔯 𝔑𝔢𝔞𝔭𝔦𝔫𝔤 𝔅𝔶=𝔞𝔫𝔡=𝔅𝔶."

BY

FLORENCE E. BURCH

Author of "No Royal Road," "A Little Boy and Girl; or, How Rollo and
Tricksy filled their Money-Box,"
&c.

THOMAS NELSON AND SONS
London, Edinburgh, and New York

1891

Contents.

I.	TOM,	7
II.	WHAT UNCLE MERRY BROUGHT,	14
III.	"GREAT" AND "GOOD,"	21
IV.	KATIE TRIES TO MAKE AMENDS,	27
V.	RIGHTEOUS INDIGNATION,	31
VI.	MIRIAM'S KNIGHT-ERRANT,	37
VII.	HAYMAKING BEGINS,	42
VIII.	KATIE'S SCHEME,	50
IX.	TOM IS IN TOO MUCH OF A HURRY,	55
X.	STRANDED HIGH AND DRY,	62
XI.	IN THE COUNTRY,	67
XII.	ALWAYS AFTER MISCHIEF,	72
XIII.	A WHITE LIE,	78
XIV.	PULLING ONIONS,	87
XV.	TOM'S GOLD MEDAL,	93
XVI.	A SAD LOSS,	100
XVII.	A LETTER TO BERMONDSEY,	107
XVIII.	MIRIAM'S WISH,	110
XIX.	KATIE'S FEAR,	110
XX.	SUSAN GIVES GOOD ADVICE,	123
XXI.	MIRIAM'S EYES ARE OPENED,	127
XXII.	TOM'S GOOD FAIRY,	132
XXIII.	AS FIRE MELTS THE DROSS AWAY,	138
XXIV.	THE NEW SCHEME,	141
XXV.	UNCLE MERRY'S BAND,	144
XXVI.	WON OVER,	149
XXVII.	A MERRY CHRISTMAS,	153
XXVIII.	"PEACE ON EARTH, GOOD WILL TOWARD MEN,"	157

DICK AND HARRY
AND TOM.

CHAPTER I.

TOM.

" Dick and Harry and Tom!
Dick and Harry and Tom!
They teased the dog and worried the cat,
And drowned the kittens in their grandfather's hat,
Did Dick and Harry and Tom."

AS the sounds died away a face appeared above the palings; and two mischievous black eyes peeped over at Miriam, who was seated on the trunk of a fallen tree with a basket of primroses on her lap.

The tree was covered with lichen, and the ground at Miriam's feet was one mass of moss and creeping ivy, primroses and wood-anemones, and all those beautiful little plants that hasten out to meet the spring. Close at hand a robin was carolling right merrily, and the plantation was full of the song of the thrushes. But Miriam scarcely heard them. She had been singing whilst she filled her basket; now she was resting and watching the anemones dancing in the sunlight that gleamed through the branches overhead.

Miriam was hardly *thinking*, but she was very much pre-occupied with some pictures that kept flitting in and out of her mind. She had been to a birthday party overnight, and she was living it all over again. Now she saw herself in her cream-coloured dress with the blue bows on it, just as it looked when she took the last peep in the glass before starting. Now she saw Katie Rivers in *her* white one, and wished she had glossy dark locks like Katie's, instead of stupid dull brown; for Katie could wear pink ribbons instead of blue. Then she saw all the happy faces on either side of the long tea-table; and again, the brilliantly-lighted drawing-room, where they had played all sorts of games. So she went on, running over all that they had said and done, until at last in imagination she was crossing to the piano, with burning cheeks, to sing "Dick and Harry and Tom." Now, although Miriam had learned this song on purpose, and practised it carefully, when it came to standing up by the piano, her heart beat so fast and her face grew so hot that she was nearly ready to cry.

Miriam remembered just how she felt; and she was pretty well convincèd that it was much nicer to sing out there in the plantation than in the drawing-room with everybody's eyes upon her. So she jumped down from her seat, and sang out clear and loud as she went on gathering her primroses; and if the birds could only have understood her language, they would all have stopped to listen to the long list of naughty things which these three young heroes did.

As it was, they only flew away when she pushed in among the branches, and went on with their own songs, as if they thought them far the prettiest.

But Miriam had not known all this while that there *was* some one listening; so it was no wonder if she was rather startled when suddenly a boy, who for some time had been peeping at her through a knot-hole, gave a shrill whistle, and jumping up, so as to get both arms on to the fence, hung there looking at her, with a broad grin on his face.

Miriam started up and dropped her basket; then, seeing who the intruder was, turned hot all over with vexation.

"*I'll* come and help pick up the primroses," called the boy, getting one leg up on the fence. "I say, though, that *was* pretty!"

Miriam was too hot to reply. She stooped down

in silence and occupied herself in gathering up the flowers.

"I say, though," shouted the boy again, "pity you didn't practise *before* the party instead of *after*."

Miriam's cheeks were getting redder and redder, but still she took no notice.

"Katie said you were ready to cry," pursued her tormentor; and a picture rose in Miriam's mind of Katie standing by the piano as cool as a cucumber while her clear, sweet voice went ringing through the room; and looking so pretty and self-possessed as she returned to her place amid the general applause.

Not that the girls withheld their applause from Miriam. They were always good-natured enough if they saw any one was nervous; but it hurt Miriam's pride to think that they only did it to encourage her. And then for Katie to go and tell it round that she was ready to cry! That was more than she could bear. "I don't care a pin what Katie says!" she exclaimed angrily; "and it's no business of yours, Tom Rivers!"

"I daresay not," said Tom, with provoking good-humour. "Tell you what *is* business of mine, though. What do you mean by telling all those fibs about me? I haven't even got a grandfather — wish I had! You could just as well say 'Bob.'"

"Bob isn't in the song," said Miriam, tossing her head.

"That's no matter," said Tom, swinging both legs over the fence and jumping down. "I don't choose to have such things sung about me; so you'd better promise, or else—"

"I'm not going to promise any such thing," said Miriam, with another toss of her head. "And you've no right in the plantation at all; it belongs to my father."

"No, it doesn't," retorted Tom; "because your father pays rent to mine for it, and I'm not going till I've punished you."

Miriam's basket was on the ground at her feet, and Tom, who by this time had approached quite close, snatched it up, and commenced swinging it about by the handle.

"Oh, don't!" cried Miriam. "You'll upset them all again."

"Promise, then," said Tom—"'Dick and Harry and *Bob!*'"

But Miriam stood out firmly.

"Can you climb a tree?" asked Tom suddenly.

"Katie can."

"Of course I could, if I chose," said Miriam.

Tom slung the basket on his arm, hugged the trunk of a big lime tree, and proceeded to draw himself up, scattering primroses as he went. When he was some height up he hooked the basket on to a twig, chose out a comfortable seat for himself, and folded his arms.

"Now!" exclaimed he.

Miriam was in a fix. It was plain that she was in Tom's power, and that sooner or later she would have to give in. She always had to in the end, when Tom took it into his head to tease—which was rather often.

"I shall tell papa," she said, after a few minutes.

Tom set to work picking little bits off the twigs and dropping them down upon her upturned face.

"I thought you could climb," said he. "Why don't you come up and get the basket? I'm not a baboon. I shouldn't hurt you; in fact, if you can get up here we won't say any more about '*Bob.*'"

"Don't they smell nice!" he went on, drawing long whiffs of their delicate scent, as Miriam made no reply. "*Ah!*"

"You'd better bring them down at once," said Miriam angrily, "or I'll go straight home and complain to papa."

"Wouldn't it like one?" said Tom in a coaxing tone; "just *one?* Open its mouth!" and picking out a beauty, he dropped it right on her face.

This was more than Miriam could stand. "I'll tell you what it is," she said: "you're a nasty, disagreeable fellow, and I hate you, Tom Rivers!"

"You might hate the man in the moon, but you couldn't get at him," jeered Tom.

"And if ever I get a chance I'll serve you out for it—*that* I will!"

"Oh! pray," cried Tom, pretending to be so frightened that he made the whole bough tremble, "what *shall* I do?" But with these words he nearly lost his balance, and leaving hold of the basket to save himself, it fell to the ground, catching among the twigs in its descent, and scattering the primroses in a shower.

Miriam picked up the basket and walked slowly away.

"I wish you'd fallen instead, and broken your neck!" she muttered as she went.

"That's a good Christian girl," Tom called after her.

Miriam knew it was not right to wish anything so dreadful, but somehow she could not help it. Tom was always teasing her, and it was no wonder if she thought him disagreeable. So when she read in her Bible, "Do good to those that despitefully use you and persecute you," she thought it hardly meant such boys as Tom.

CHAPTER II.

WHAT UNCLE MERRY BROUGHT.

IF Tom had not a grandfather, Miriam had a great-*uncle*. In fact her chief object in taking her primrose-basket out into the plantation that morning had been to make the house look bright with flowers, for Great-uncle Merry was expected to dinner.

Miriam had got so angry with Tom that she positively forgot all about this until she got right indoors and smelt the fragrant scent of baking. There was always a special kind of cake made on these occasions, and it was just that minute out of the oven.

The smell of baking brought Uncle Merry to mind at once—but not the flowers. Miriam's thoughts, which were in the habit of flying very rapidly, were too often directed upon her own interests. Her great-uncle never came without bringing her a present, and she was so absorbed in wondering what it would be this time that it had quite slipped her mind how pretty she had meant to make his welcome. Selfishness is a wonderfully rampant weed.

"I know what I should *like*," said Miriam to herself, flinging down the basket and running to the dining-room to see the time.

"Miss Miriam!" called Susan from the kitchen door.

Miriam gave a hasty glance at the timepiece and hurried out. "Just time to change my frock," she said to herself as she went.

"Your mamma has got all the glasses in here, Miss Miriam," said Susan, as she appeared.

"How *lovely* that cake smells!" cried Miriam.— "Glasses! *what* glasses, Sue?"

Miriam's mother answered. "For the primroses," replied she from within; "and I want you to come at once and arrange them for me. You will just have time."

Miriam's countenance fell.

"But where are they?" continued her mother, on seeing her empty hands. "Haven't you brought any, after all?"

"I *did* pick a *lot*," answered Miriam, beginning to turn red—"a whole basketful."

"And left them behind?"

"It was that nasty boy Tom Rivers," answered Miriam, looking down. "I hate him! and I wish he'd fallen instead of the basket, and broken his neck." And thereupon she related how Tom had teased her about her song and carried off her primroses up the tree. "I wish he'd killed himself!" repeated Miriam.

"Gently, gently!" interposed mamma. "I hardly think you would be glad to see your friend Katie in such terrible trouble."

"I shouldn't care," said Miriam. "Katie's every bit as bad as Tom. It was Katie told him I was ready to cry, and that was what made Tom tease me. I hate them *both*." And away she skulked, with a face as black as pitch; so Susan had to carry back the flower-glasses empty.

Half-an-hour later the hall was resounding with Great-uncle Merry's voice, which was as cheery as his name; and Miriam was tugging him out of his overcoat, dying with curiosity to know what was in the pockets, and wishing she might poke about in them to see. But Great-uncle Merry had his own ideas about such things. Perhaps he thought patience was a good sauce for enjoyment; or perhaps he wanted to make sure that it was *himself* and not the present that Miriam was so glad to see. Anyhow, not until his watch began to warn him it was time to think of going home did Uncle Merry say a word upon the subject.

Miriam was perched upon the arm of Great-uncle Merry's chair, and he was playing with her hair.

"Oh, don't go yet," cried Miriam, as he felt for his chain. "Perhaps if you weren't to look at the watch the hands would stop." And Miriam tried to hide it between her palms. But Great-uncle Merry shook his head.

"If the hands stop, time won't," said he sagely, rattling his bunch of seals; so Miriam had to give it up.

"Ten minutes more, and then I'm off," said Great-uncle Merry. "But, by-the-by, I haven't said a word of what I've brought for you. Now guess."

"A pocket full of air," said Miriam saucily.

Great-uncle Merry made a face, declaring himself half a mind to let her abide by her guess. But Miriam begged and prayed so that his dear old heart was softened.

"What do you want most of all?" asked he.

Miriam thought a minute, then made as if to speak, but held her tongue, as though she didn't like to say.

"Well," said Uncle Merry, "time's half up."

Miriam clasped her hands. "O Uncle Merry, I *did* want a lovely gold locket like Katie were last night," said she, in her most coaxing way.

"You *did?*" said Uncle Merry. "Just like all the lasses, full of vanity! Well, let's see what I've got;" and after fumbling mysteriously in his waistcoat pocket he drew out a bright new half-sovereign. "Now you can please yourself," said he. "Mind you spend it well."

Miriam threw her arms around his neck and fairly smothered him. "Oh, you dear old Uncle Merry!" she began. But Uncle Merry shook her off and went to get his coat.

Meanwhile Tom had gone home to tell Katie what a pet Miriam was in about the primroses.

Now Tom was not altogether bad, only he had a sad love of teasing. He had only intended to plague Miriam a little at first about the song; but when she turned so red he could not resist the temptation of jumping over the palings and carrying off her basket. Even then he did not mean to leave it up the tree, and upsetting it was quite an accident. But when Miriam lost her temper and got so angry, Tom altogether forgot that he was in the wrong, and he felt very proud of himself up there, swinging his legs and whistling, as he watched her out of the plantation. Then he got out his knife, and cut his name on the tree.

At last, after waiting a long while to see if Miriam would come back as soon as she fancied he was gone, he began to get cold and hungry; so he shut his knife up with a click and descended.

"Wasn't she *wild!*" said he to himself, as he

stepped over the heap of primroses and made for the palings; "and won't Katie laugh!"

But Katie didn't laugh. "O Tom," she exclaimed, "how could you be so unkind? You ought to go right back and gather another basketful for her."

"Catch me," laughed Tom. "How red she got, though!"

"I think it was very mean of you," said Katie. "You knew she couldn't get the basket if you put it up there. It wasn't kind to tease her about her song either."

"All very fine," retorted Tom. "Who told me she was ready to cry?"

"But I didn't intend to tease her about it," said Katie; "and I clapped my hands till they smarted."

"You're just like a girl," said Tom, turning on his heel. "They're like weathercocks. They go whichever way the wind blows. That's why boys can't play with them."

"O Tom," cried Katie, "I learned to climb trees and jump ditches on purpose to be able to play with *you*, and I always stand up for you; now, don't I?"

"What's the use of *that?*" snarled Tom. "As if I was a baby, and wanted any one to stand up for *me!*" and off he stalked to examine his new rabbit-hutch, looking very big. But in reality Tom felt rather small; for he cared a good deal about Katie's opinion, and it spoilt the fun of teasing Miriam to think that Katie didn't approve. He didn't half enjoy the new rabbit-hutch all alone either; so he went to peep in at the stable door, and startled the pony by calling, "Gee-up!" Then he marched off to the poultry-yard, and amused himself by making the hens believe that he was going to feed them; and when they came tiptoe, stretching up their necks to see what he had got for them, he opened his hand and showed that it was empty.

At last, however, they found out that he was only making fun of them, and declined to take any further notice; so Tom had to think of something else to do. But he took good care to keep out of Katie's way till dinner-time.

CHAPTER III.

"*GREAT*" AND "*GOOD.*"

IMMEDIATELY after dinner Katie slipped round to Tom's side. "Let's go in the woods, Tom," whispered she. "I do so want to get some violets down by the brook. We can cross on the stones, like we did last time."

But Tom grumbled something about not being in the humour.

Katie began to coax. "O Tom," begged she, "the Easter holidays will be up the day after tomorrow, you know, and it may rain to-morrow. You had the rabbit-hutch to paint yesterday; but now that's done, and looks so nice, you might go."

Tom would have said yes at once if it had not been for what Katie had said about Miriam; however, he brightened up when she began to praise the rabbit-hutch. "I must feed the rabbits first," said he.

Katie skipped off to get her hat, without waiting for any further answer; and in a very short space of time they were on their road, as good friends as ever.

The way they chose led from the farm-yard across some fields, and through a little copse on the hillside to the brook, beyond which lay the woods. There were plenty of anemones in the copse, and a good many violets peeping out in little clusters from amongst the grass. But Katie did not want to stop for these, so they pushed on.

The hazel bushes grew thicker and more tangled the nearer they were to the brook, and swished their long green catkins in Katie's face as she tried to keep up with Tom. This was no easy matter, for they caught her dress and held her back; but she fought bravely on until they arrived at the hurdle fence. Katie drew a long breath.

"Now for it," said Tom, placing his hand on the top bar.

"Once, twice, thrice!" cried Katie, and in less than a minute they were on the other side.

"Not many girls can do like that," said Tom, with an air of pride. "You're as good as a boy to go out with."

The brook was low, for it was dry weather; so they got down and walked along on the pebbles, with the high banks towering up above them, and the willows overhead reaching down their gray tufts as if they longed for a dip in the clear bright stream. Here and there the bed of the brook was so narrow and muddy that they had to clamber up again;

which was rather a difficult undertaking, because the bank had been washed away in winter when the stream was swollen with the melted snow, and it was by no means easy to get a foothold.

The worst place of all was where the copse came to an end, and the brook flowed on between two fields. The water was quite deep here; and a ditch, surmounted by a hedge, stood between them and the field. Fortunately, however, in the hedge was a gap, which had merely been stopped up with a hurdle. They had only to leap the ditch and climb the bank, and it would be easy to get over.

"Forward!" shouted Tom, suiting the action to the word. "Into the trench and scale the ramparts!"

Katie obeyed the word of command; and after a few slips and a little scrambling they conquered the difficulty, and were soon half-way up the field; then across the brook, where some flat stones made a regular ford, and into the wood.

Here the ground was studded with the delicate blossoms of the primrose and wood-anemone, peeping out from among their pale green leaves, and clustering around the roots of the trees as if they loved the dear old friends who had cast such a warm mantle over them during the winter frost. Katie began gathering at once, whilst Tom dug up some roots with his knife, and then set to work at his favourite occupation of cutting his initials on a tree.

As soon as her basket was full, Katie came and looked over Tom, who was just finishing the R.

"How big you've made the letters, Tom!" she cried.

"They won't grow up in a hurry," observed Tom, twisting his head on one side, and stepping back a little to see the effect. "It's like making your mark in the world. Our usher says that if you want to do that you mustn't be afraid of work, because only great actions bring lasting fame."

Tom looked as if he had said something very grand, as he put his knife in his pocket; but Katie's face wore a thoughtful expression.

"Our governess says it doesn't so much matter about being great," she said, "as long as we're good."

"That's all very well for girls," said Tom; "but it wouldn't do for boys and men—soldiers for instance. Soldiers have to be brave, and do *great* things."

"Only Miss Ansell says the little things show what we're made of," rejoined Katie; "and that if we're made of the right stuff we shall be brave without thinking about it, when there's any need."

Miss Ansell was quite right, and Katie had understood exactly what she meant. If boys and girls are made of the true metal they will grow up to be like good tools, ready for use whenever the Master's hand has need of them; and the only way to be "faithful in that which is greatest" is to be "faithful in that which is least."

"Do girls ever cut their initials on trees?" asked Katie presently.

"I don't think they do," said Tom; "but *you* might, because you can climb almost like a boy—only don't break my new knife."

Katie laughed and took the knife in her hand; and after some pains, and a very little assistance, soon succeeded in carving a very creditable "K R"—though the K looked rather as if it had a mind to kick the R round to the other side of the trunk.

Then they went on again to the bank where the violets grew; and by the time they had gathered enough, the sun warned them that it was time to go home; so they turned back, Tom carrying the roots, and Katie the flowers.

They had decided upon returning a different way, which would bring them home by the lane that led past the plantation, because Katie wanted some small-leafed ivy off the fence. Tom's knife had to come out again to strip it off, it clung so tightly to the wood; meanwhile Katie amused herself with peeping over.

"I wish we lived here," said she. "It would be so nice to play at wild Indians all among these big trees. And oh! look, Tom—there's such a beauty has been blown down. It will be chopped up for faggots now. What a pity!" (It was the very one Miriam had been sitting on that morning.)

"My name is up that one," said Tom, pointing to the lime tree, "ever so high."

"Is it?" cried Katie, who was always proud of Tom's achievements. "When did you do it?"

"This morning," said Tom, suddenly remembering about Miriam.

"Oh—" said Katie, who remembered too.

When they got opposite the garden gate Katie stopped. "Tom," said she, "I've a lot more primroses than I shall want. Shall we go and give Miriam some?"

"She can get plenty in the plantation," said Tom.

"But we might give her some of these," said Katie.

"I don't see why we should pick flowers for *her*," grumbled Tom.

"But you know," began Katie, "you upset—"

"Well, she shouldn't have been in such a temper," interrupted Tom, who, to tell the truth, was heartily ashamed of himself, though he was too proud to own it.

But Katie persisted.

"I should like to give her some, if you wouldn't mind going on without me," said she.

"All very fine," grumbled Tom, as the gate swung after her. "I went on purpose to please you, and now I'm to go home by myself."

CHAPTER IV.

KATIE TRIES TO MAKE AMENDS.

MIRIAM was just returning from the henhouse with a basket of new-laid eggs for Great-uncle Merry, when Katie ran up the path calling, "Miriam, I've brought you some primroses."

Miriam walked slowly towards her.

"Who said I wanted any primroses?" she asked sullenly.

"I thought you would be sure to like some," replied Katie. "We've been into the wood for them, and I don't want more than half of what we've gathered. See what a quantity! Aren't they lovely?"

"They're very pretty," said Miriam, who would really have liked some for her great-uncle to take home with him. "But I don't want them. I can get plenty. They're common enough."

Katie thought this a very ungracious way of receiving her offer; but she was determined to be good-natured.

"Won't you have some violets?" she asked; "they're sweet-smelling ones."

"Mamma doesn't like them in the house," replied Miriam; "they make her head ache. No, thank you, Kate; I won't rob you."

"You wouldn't be robbing me," Katie assured her; "I gathered plenty on purpose, because I knew you were fond of them, and—I wanted to make up for Tom being so rude this morning," she added.

"What difference will *your* violets make to that?" said Miriam disdainfully. "I've no doubt you've both been laughing about it. Anyhow, I don't suppose Tom is sorry, is he?"

Katie couldn't truthfully say she thought he was.

"I don't want any flowers that Tom has picked," Miriam went on; "nor yet any that *you've* picked either, for you're just as bad."

"Miriam!" cried Katie, "*I* never tease you."

"You told Tom I was ready to cry at the party," said Miriam angrily. "But I don't care for either of you; and I can't stay talking now, because mamma is waiting for these eggs for Great-uncle Merry;" and so saying, off she marched, leaving Katie in the middle of the path.

Katie turned and walked slowly back.

Tom was still outside the gate waiting for her.

"Hullo!" cried he; "wouldn't she have 'em? Ho!

isn't she proud? I tell you, Katie, it's of no use troubling about her; only you're just like a girl."

"But you *were* in the wrong, Tom," said his sister, "so it's for us to try and make it up. Perhaps she'd have taken them if you'd gone with me and said you were sorry."

"I wasn't going to do *that*," said Tom doggedly.

It was plain argument would do no good; so Katie dropped the subject, and Tom stalked on in dignified silence a step or two ahead, swinging his bundle of roots and whistling.

This was not a very nice ending to their happy afternoon. Katie almost wished she had not persisted in offering Miriam the flowers, since it had made matters rather worse than better. This Katie was a peace-loving little maiden, and she was racking her brains to think what she could say to bring Tom round. She was just about to speak, when a sudden hue and cry some little way behind made them both turn sharply round.

A small boy, barefoot and bareheaded, was tearing full speed down the road after them; and some fifteen or twenty yards behind, but rapidly gaining on him, was another bigger boy, with a stout stick in his hand.

"That's Dick Bull at his tricks again," cried Tom, forgetting all about Miriam and the flowers. "Hi! stop there! stop, I say!"

But Dick showed no signs of paying any heed.

"Stop there!" shouted Tom again, taking a step or two out to meet him, and holding up his hand. But Dick only grinned savagely, and swung the stick around his head, as much as to say, "Keep clear!"

He was now almost close upon the poor fugitive, whose face was crimson with terror and exertion. A minute more and he would be within reach. The wretched child, who was not much more than half his size, seemed to feel Dick's breath upon his neck. He turned to cast a terrified backward glance, swerved sideways, and, tripping on a little heap of turf cutting, fell full length, with his arms before him, and his face in a bed of nettles.

Dick uttered a yell of delight, and rushing forward, seized upon the poor wretch and fell to belabouring him unmercifully with the stick. But now was Tom's time to show his mettle. Flinging aside his bundle of roots, he sprang across the road, and seized the young ruffian by the collar.

CHAPTER V.

RIGHTEOUS INDIGNATION.

DICK BULL was a year older than Tom, and a size bigger—a lad with the making of a bully in him. But Tom didn't stop to think about that. All he knew was that poor, half-witted little Tim—Dick's step-brother—was on the ground, with his face in a bed of nettles; and that no boy with a grain of pluck in him ought to stand by and see a fellow knocked about when he was down.

"Come off him!" shouted he, tugging with might and main at Dick's collar. "Let him get up, or you shall be sorry!"

"You dare to interfere," bellowed Dick, without relaxing hold. "It's no business of yours. Hold off, or I'll let you know it." And slashing round with his stick, Dick caught Tom such a blow across the knuckles as brought the water to his eyes.

"Stop that!" cried Tom, "and let him be, I say." And with a tremendous effort he pulled Dick off and threw him down on the ground.

But Dick was up in an instant, and turned upon him savagely. "What business have you to meddle?" yelled he, squaring up to Tom.

"What business have you to ill-use that poor fellow?" said Tom, getting between him and his step-brother. "Let him go home, or I'll have you sent to jail for it."

"Get out of my way, or I'll smash your head in!" roared Dick. "I'll fight you, and teach you to mind what don't concern you."

"O Tom!" cried Katie in alarm, "*don't* fight." But Tom's jacket was already off.

"I'm not afraid of *you*," said he to Dick, rolling up his sleeves. "You're bigger than I am, but you're a coward, or you wouldn't be so mean as to ill-use a boy that can't defend himself."

"He should learn to mind what I say," retorted Dick; "and if he hasn't got wits enough to learn any other way, he must be taught with a stick."

"I'll give you a thrashing first," threatened Tom stoutly, "or take it myself."

"Come on, then!" yelled Dick, throwing away his stick, and rushing forward with such a tremendous blow at Tom's chest that Tom staggered backward, and for the instant all the breath seemed gone out of his body.

Dick uttered a jeering laugh, thinking he had given Tom his quietus. "That's a taste for you," said he, making towards him again, "and I don't recommend—"

But before he could finish Tom had recovered, and was up and at him; and for several seconds blows on both sides fell fast and thick.

Tom, like most other boys, had had his share of fighting to do at school, though he was not one to seek a quarrel. He knew how to guard and parry; but Dick fought with the desperateness of a bully, and before long Tom's face was getting pretty well knocked about.

Katie looked on in terrible distress, whilst Tim, who by this time had got up out of the nettles, had gathered himself together for a run, and was making the best of a speedy retreat, crying and rubbing his blistered face as he went.

Meanwhile Tom's blood was too much up to let him heed his bruises. He began to wonder, though, how much longer he could hold out, for he was getting terribly out of breath. But suddenly Tom thought of a manœuvre he had seen done at school. All in a minute, just as Dick drew in his fist to launch one of his terrific blows, Katie saw Tom duck his head and rush forward, closing with Dick in a desperate embrace. For a short time they hugged and tussled, and swayed and wrestled, Dick threatening every minute to crush the breath out of his slighter adversary; but just when it seemed as if, by sheer force of superior weight, Dick must press him down to the ground, Tom himself suddenly stooped, thrust one leg forward, gripped Dick below the centre of gravity, and before he knew what was happening, had him sprawling on the ground.

"There!" said he. " Perhaps that'll teach you that it doesn't always do to bully boys who are smaller than yourself."

Then picking up his jacket, and beckoning Katie to follow, Tom turned homeward, leaving the fallen braggart to pick himself up.

Meanwhile Tom was at leisure to examine his own knuckles, which were considerably cut and bruised.

"How does my face look, Katie?" he asked, turning full towards her.

Poor tender-hearted Katie was horrified at his appearance; but bad as that was, Tom looked ten times worse an hour afterwards, when, having related the story of his encounter, and got his bruises bandaged with raw beef, he sat down to tea.

"I never beat a fellow with so much satisfaction," said he, though, as he fell to work on the bread and butter; for between the excursion to the woods, and the fight with Dick, and the delay consequent on bathing and dressing his damaged head and hands, Tom's appetite was pretty keen.

Mrs. Rivers was inclined to look rather seriously at it.

"I don't like your getting into fights with boys of Dick's sort," said she.

"But I guess you wouldn't have liked to see me stand by, mother, and let him flog Tim," returned the young hero. "That's a thing I *couldn't* do," added Tom with conviction; "and I fancy I've given him a lesson he won't forget in a hurry."

"Was he much hurt?" Katie asked.

"Not more than he deserved," answered Tom promptly. "I made sure of that before I came away. You always do, you know," added Tom, with an air of importance that caused his mother to smile in spite of herself, "when you fight a fellow. But you can see at a glance if he's really damaged," he concluded. "Dick was only humbled."

"I don't *like* fighting," Tom confided to Katie afterwards. "But there *is* such a thing as righteous indignation, you know, and when that gets hold of a fellow he *has* to fight."

"Like the old knights used to," said Katie admiringly.

"Only they used to fight on horseback," said Tom; "and it was generally on behalf of some girl or other. Nobody was thought anything of who wasn't ready to give his life for a girl."

Katie's thoughts reverted to Miriam in the plantation, and she couldn't help wondering what would have been the verdict in those chivalrous old times on a boy who should behave as rudely to a girl as Tom had done to her.

But as regarded the effect of the lesson he had taught Dick, Tom *was* mistaken, and Dick was only the more spiteful to his afflicted little step-brother for the defeat he had sustained at the hands of Tim's champion.

Meanwhile Tom's knuckles healed, and the bruises on his face turned from black to green, and from green to brown, until by the end of the week it was doubtful whether there would be much trace of them left to show to the boys at school by the following Monday.

CHAPTER VI.

MIRIAM'S KNIGHT-ERRANT.

TOM saw no more of Dick Bull before the holidays were up, partly because for the first two days he himself was such an unsightly object that he preferred not showing his face to the general public, and partly because if Dick had chanced to see Tom coming in his direction he would have got out of the way in double-quick time.

In the meanwhile Tom had another opportunity of exercising his disposition to chivalry.

Saturday turned out such a beautiful day that, after a due inspection of his looking-glass, Tom declared he should hang about the garden no longer. Unfortunately, however, Katie had to stay indoors, because the dressmaker was coming to see about some alterations in a dress which did not sit quite right; so Tom had to go by himself.

Fact was, Tom had grown heartily tired of the garden. For the first day or two the stiff, swollen state of his face had kept reminding him that he was a bit of a hero; and of course heroes do different things from ordinary people. But as the bruises healed Tom gradually descended from his pedestal, and became once more an ordinary sort of individual. First he grew impatient about the ugly green patches; then he grew callous whether people thought them ornamental or not; finally he arrived at the conclusion that it was "like a girl" to stay in for the sake of his appearance. So grasping his stick in one hand, and thrusting the other in his trousers pocket, he set off at a brisk pace to enjoy the west wind and the sunshine, still looking rather unsightly, but whistling a lively tune.

Passing the plantation, Tom's tune changed, and he began whistling "Dick and Harry and Tom," just as he had heard Miriam sing it as she sat upon the fallen tree; for Tom was quick at catching up a tune.

"I wonder if she's there this morning," said Tom to himself, clambering up to the palings to peep over.

The flowers, all withered and dead, were lying at the foot of the tree; but Miriam was nowhere to be seen.

"I don't believe she's been here since," said Tom to himself. "That's just like Miriam." But Tom half wished in the bottom of his heart that he hadn't done it. The flowers looked so sad; they seemed to reproach him.

"If it had not been for you," they seemed to say, "we might still have been adorning the house with our beauty and fragrance."

Ah, what lovely flowers of peace and happiness we may destroy by unkind words or acts! and how anxious we should be to "scatter seeds of kindness for our reaping by-and-by!"

Tom hung there on the palings some time, half inclined to get over and climb the lime tree to see how his initials looked; but he changed his mind. In the field at the further end of the plantation was a pond where he often went to catch tadpoles and water-newts; and thither Tom directed his steps. The pond lay in a deep hollow, hidden by a group of firs and larches, and fringed by a thick tangle of bramble and furze, now all golden with bloom. Tom pushed the gate open, went straight across the grass to a gap where the bushes had been cut away for the cattle to go down and drink, and began to poke about in the water with his stick. But there were no tadpoles to be seen. He was just turning away, when he heard a great splash at the other side, and glancing across, whom should he see but Miriam, with one foot in the water, clinging tightly with both hands to an overhanging bough, her dress held fast by the hooked thorns of the dog-rose brambles.

"Hold on till I come," cried Tom, elbowing his

way in among the furze bushes. "Hold tight! If the other foot slips you'll be done for."

"Don't come near me!" screamed Miriam, turning scarlet, and struggling to get her dress free. "I can get out quite well by myself. It's all your fault I slipped. You've come on purpose to plague me."

"I didn't know you were here till I heard your foot go splash," called Tom. "Hold on! I'm coming to help you. I'm your knight-errant."

The bank was so slippery that Tom was afraid he would never reach Miriam in time. He crushed through the brambles, regardless of consequences; but the tangle was so thick that it was hard work to make any progress.

"How *did* you get there?" exclaimed he.

But Miriam was struggling too hard to answer, and just as Tom was almost within arm's length, by a desperate effort she regained her footing and tore her dress free.

"How you've hurt your hands!" cried Tom.

They were all scratched and bleeding. There were some dreadful rents, too, in her frock, which was all splashed and muddy. But Miriam was so vexed that she hardly felt the smart. "I don't care," cried she; "I would rather scratch them a hundred times over than be helped by you, for you're a nasty, disagreeable boy, and my papa is going to give you a good talking to."

"You don't suppose *I* care for that!" retorted Tom contemptuously, turning away and preparing to push his way back through the furze. "And I'll see you drown, another time, before I'll offer to help you."

"What a horrid-tempered thing she is!" he said to himself, as he crossed the grass; "and how glad I am that I didn't tell her I was sorry!" And off he strode, feeling very much Miriam's superior.

"I say, though, *you* began it all," said Tom's conscience.

"Well, she had no need to be so cross because I quizzed her a little," urged Tom in self-defence.

"But when you saw she didn't like it, the kindest and most Christian thing would have been to drop it at once," expostulated the tiresome little monitor.

"She's only a girl after all," said Tom, "and girls *are* silly—all except Katie. I shouldn't wonder a bit if she doesn't even know what a knight-errant is;" for Tom was a little sore that his knight-errantry had been rejected. "As to her father, I don't care *that* for *him!*" And Tom snapped his fingers and broke out whistling. Nevertheless, he chose a way home that didn't lead him past Mr. Grayson's, thereby proving the truth of the good old saying that "conscience makes cowards of us all."

CHAPTER VII.

HAYMAKING BEGINS.

THE early spring flowers died, and the orchards showered down their pink and white snow. Then the cuckoo came; the meadows grew golden with buttercups, and farmers watched the waving grass until the gold, too, died out of it, and left it brown and purple with the ripening seed—ready for the scythe. Then dog-roses began to peep out in the hedges; the cuckoo's note grew uncertain; and bands of men, hot and travel-stained, trudged along the roads and lanes with scythes over their shoulders and whetstones strapped to their waistbelts.

All through this lovely spring-time Miriam had scarcely spoken to Katie.

Katie had made more than one attempt at a reconciliation. She had tried to wait for Miriam coming out of school, as she always used to. She had started early to waylay her by the end of the plantation; she had offered her pencil when the point of Miriam's broke; and, in short, had done a hundred and one things to show her that she wanted to be friends. But all her overtures of peace were rejected. Miriam always managed to be looking the other way when Katie tried to speak to her; and immediately school was over she always linked arms with some other girl, and went off whispering, to show Katie that she was not wanted.

Meanwhile haymaking had commenced.

It was late afternoon when Mr. Grayson's haymakers arrived. Their faces were scorched and sunburnt, and they dragged their feet wearily as they came up the yard. They had been on the tramp since three that morning; for, like many haymakers, they came from a distance.

Mr. Grayson was indoors at tea when they arrived, but he went out at once to speak to them, and Miriam soon followed. These men had cut her father's grass for many seasons, and had watched her grow up from a tiny baby. In the meantime Mrs. Grayson had gone to the kitchen to see about ordering some refreshment for them, and when they had quenched their thirst on the huge cans of tea which she sent out, and satisfied their hunger on the bread and cheese, they were glad to have a wash at the pump, and stretch themselves upon the hay in the loft where they were to pass the night. Long before the shadows fell they were sleeping the sleep of exhausted nature, so as to be up and at work with the first peep of day.

The sun was not yet down when another man came up the yard.

Miriam was just returning from the garden, where she had been gathering gooseberries for preserving, and she stopped against the kitchen door to look at him. He was very lame and footsore, but he touched his hat and hobbled quickly forward on seeing Miriam. "Beg pardon, missie," said he; "is the genelman a-goin' to cut his hay?"

"They are going to begin to-morrow," replied Miriam, who had retreated a step or two inside. "But papa has got all the men he wants."

The man slowly took the scythe down off his shoulder, and rested the handle on the ground, so that he could support his weight on it; then he lifted one foot stiffly on to the doorstep, and pushed his hat back on his forehead.

"Maybe he could do with another hand, missie," pleaded he, "to get his grass up quick. It's a long spell of fine weather we've been havin', and it's been powerful hot to-day. Might come a storm afore he got it carried, and spoil it all. Maybe you'd ask him, missie."

Miriam didn't altogether like the look of the man. She misinterpreted the traces of fatigue and poverty. "I can *ask*," said she; "but I know it's of no use."

"You see, sir," the man said, when Mr. Grayson came out, which he did pretty quickly on hearing that Miriam had left a rough-looking stranger waiting at the unguarded door—"you see, sir, I've tramped from Lunnon every single step to-day, and I ha'n't got a penny about me; and unless so be as I get work to-night I don't know what I'm to do; and I'm that footsore I can hardly get along."

But to give him work was out of Mr. Grayson's power, for he had already fully as many hands as his field would require, and he told the poor fellow so.

"However," he added kindly, "you can at any rate sit down on the bench yonder and have a rest and a meal, to carry you on your way a bit." And he at once went indoors to find his wife. Meanwhile the poor wayworn man had reached the bench, and leaned his back against the wall.

"Ah, what a blessed thing rest is!" exclaimed he, stretching his legs out before him as Mr. Grayson disappeared. " That genelman's a Christian, if there *is* one to be found; and there ain't many like him. The most on 'em just gives you your answer, and off you must go—starve or die!"

An hour later, by Mr. Grayson's advice, he stood outside Mr. Rivers's back door, and shortly afterwards he was tasting the delight of a clean straw bed in an outhouse in the stable-yard—rolling himself up for a good night's sleep, in the happy prospect of several days' work and corresponding pay.

Katie was surprised, on waking next morning, to hear the "slish, slish" of the scythes in the grass, and the ring of the whetstone on the blade.

"I *do* believe it's our field, too," said she, putting her tangled mane round Tom's door, after trying repeatedly to rouse him from the outside. "You just hark!"

Tom sprang up, sitting in his bed. "You're not up, Kit, are you?" exclaimed he, digging his knuckles into his eyes to get them open.

Katie shook her head, which was certainly a degree rougher than it would be after the application of a brush and comb. "I shan't be long, though," said she. "Make haste, Tom; I'm *certain* it's our field." And gently pulling Tom's door to, away she pattered with her bare pink feet.

A short time after, the two crept downstairs, undid the bolts, and slipping out into the fresh morning air, sped down the field way, and away to the meadow.

Yes, Katie was quite right. The man had been at work an hour already. There was a good broad strip mown. "And papa never told us!" exclaimed Katie.

The man was just straightening himself up to

whet his scythe. Seeing Tom and Katie, he put a forefinger up to the brim of his hat, and wished them a civil good-morning.

"We didn't know you were coming," said Tom, stepping across the new-cut grass with his hands in his pockets.

"Nor I nuther, sir, till after you was in bed, I reckon," returned the man; and he related how he had been sent on by Mr. Grayson to try his luck at getting work there.

Tom asked where he came from, and was told "Lunnon."

"Have you been in Lunnon, sir?" asked the man.

Tom replied that he had once or twice.

"It's a big place, if you was to set out to walk from one end of it to t'other," continued the man; "but when you come to tramp right out here—my word, it's a stiffish job."

"What part do you live in?" asked Tom.

"In what they call Bermondsey, sir," replied the man. "It ain't a nice part, specially the court what we live in—close and dirty, like. Now this—" and as he looked round about him his soul seemed to drink its fill of the loveliness—the verdure and the sunshine, and the sweetness of the summer morning. "This *is* beautiful," he went on. "I tell you what. I said my prayers this morning, when I come out o' that 'ere shed, for the first time this many a day—not on my knees, like; I couldn't wait for that. I ses, ses I, 'O God, this 'ere's a beautiful world to 'a' made!—and Lord send my little Tab may come to see it one o' these days;' and I believe he will."

The man was going on whetting his scythe; but Katie, who until then had been standing on the pathway near the hedge, now picked her way across the grass, regardless of the dew. "Who is *Tab?*" asked she, looking up in his face.

"Tab's the eldest o' my two children, little miss," replied the man, with his eyes still on his blade though; and Katie thought she saw the glisten of something like tears in them.

"Poor little Tab! turned twelve she is, this month, miss, and you wouldn't think she was more than eight."

"Is she ill?" asked Katie next.

"Deformed," the man replied. "A drunken woman dropped her when she were a little mite not more'n two days old; and that's what come of it. It hurt the spine, you see, and she grew hump-backed. But with as sweet a face as any angel in a pictur', miss," he went on, as Katie, hardly knowing what to say to such a grievous tale, stood silent, looking on the grass.

"And she's never seen the country, I suppose?" said Katie, looking up again.

Tab's father shook his head. "Never been outside the court where she first saw daylight, miss," answered he—"such daylight as it is. And there she sets and works all day up in our little garret along o' Zillah—that's the other one, miss; and which o' those two works the hardest 'd puzzle any one to say."

Katie inquired what they worked at.

The man replied, "At mending dolls. Zill buys 'em cheap from ragmen and the like, and then they mend their clothes and *titiwate* 'em up for me to wheel out on my barrow for to sell."

Katie's interest was thoroughly awakened. She asked a lot of questions about this dollies' hospital. The occupation by which Tab and Zillah earned their bread was a branch of industry that she had never heard of.

"But I must get on with my work afore the sun gets high," Tab's father said, with a look round at the eastern sky; "the dew's a-dryin' up a'ready;" and he fell to work again.

Tom and Katie watched awhile, then they walked away. Tom cleaned and fed his rabbits, while Katie raked and watered her garden bed. But everywhere the distant "slish, slish" of the mower's scythe followed them with its strange fascination, and they could not keep away from the field.

CHAPTER VIII.

KATIE'S SCHEME.

"TOM!" said Katie, as the two children went upstairs that evening after having their supper of plain seed-cake and new milk—"Tom, do look at Tab's father."

Katie's head was out of the casement, and Tab's father, hearing her voice, looked up.

He was seated on the chopping-stool, where he had eaten his supper after coming up from the field. Katie nodded, and called "Good-night;" and the man, touching his hat respectfully, got up and moved off towards the shed for his night's rest. "He was looking *so* happy!" exclaimed Katie, as Tom came and leaned on the sill beside her.

"I expect he was jolly hungry for his supper," remarked he.

"I wonder if he was saying his prayers again?" said Katie thoughtfully, remembering what Tab's father had said that morning.

"It's a rum fashion of doing it, if he was," observed Tom, "staring at the sky, with his big knife in his hand and his mouth full."

To Tom's mind *kneeling* made up a good deal of the rightness of prayers; yet probably the unspoken thankfulness of this poor man, who believed that it was *God* who had directed him to this job of work and sent him his good meal—as he cares for the sparrows—was far more well-pleasing in the heavenly Father's sight than many a form of words which educated Christians gabble over, night and morning, on their knees.

Katie had an inkling of this truth. "He was looking right out there," said she, pointing where the setting sun had left a bright gold band along the horizon. "It made him think of heaven, I believe; and very likely he was wishing Tab could see it too."

Tom said, "Perhaps," and a few minutes later they went to their rooms; but long after Tom was sound asleep, Katie lay awake maturing a plan that had come into her head whilst she knelt beside her bed. Katie heard ten o'clock strike that night— a very unusual thing for her to do.

The consequence was that Tom roused first next morning, and Katie had a scramble to get dressed before he went downstairs.

"Tom!" cried she, hurrying after him as he set off running towards the field, "*do* stop a bit; I've got a plan."

The plan was this: it had struck Katie that she and Tom might do what boys and girls in other towns and villages were doing—start a fresh-air mission at their own expense, and give poor Tab and Zillah two or three weeks' outing in the country. "They would enjoy it so," said she.

Tom stopped short and thrust his stick into the hedge—a way he had when he couldn't quite see to the bottom of anything. "That's just like a girl's idea," objected he; "you don't consider what it would cost!"

Katie inquired *how* much he thought, and Tom replied with the important monosyllable, "Gold." But Katie was not dismayed.

"I thought of asking all the girls at school to help—all except Miriam, of course; it's of no use asking her. She spent her half-sovereign on that gold locket she's so proud of, and she never gives away a penny. But if all the rest gave ever so little, we could manage it."

The scheme took with the girls beyond Katie's fondest expectations; and although, on admitting Mrs. Rivers to their confidence, it was found that more money would be required than even Tom had supposed, contributions poured in so readily that before the hay was carried a sufficient sum was already in hand.

"Miriam *will* be wild when she hears what

we've done," observed Tom, who of course was present at the committee meeting. The girls had all come up to the hay-making, and had tea out in the orchard. "But she doesn't deserve to know—nasty, proud young minx!"

"And what's more," added another, "we don't mean her to."

"You see," said Katie, who didn't feel quite comfortable about Miriam's being out of it, "we *can't* ask her, for she won't give us a chance." For Miriam never spoke to Katie now.

"Oh! let her go on putting all her money in the savings-bank to buy jewellery with," sneered Tom. "We've got enough without her."

It was a good deal later than usual that night when Tom and Katie went upstairs to bed. They had ridden up from the field on the last load of hay, and accompanied their little friends down the lane as far as the plantation; and now the great, broad moon was shining full in at the casement on the staircase.

Katie stopped a moment to look out. "There goes Tab's father," said she. He was just going off to his bed in the out-house. "He's tired, *I* know," added Katie. "But didn't he just look glad when we told him about our scheme; and how pleased the girls all were with him!"

Tom nodded. "Say, Kit," said he, "it was just

like a girl to hit on such a scheme. Boys never seem to think of doing other people good."

"Girls can't be '*knight-errants,*' anyhow," said Katie, who always wanted to find something to say for everybody. "I don't see, though, why boys shouldn't think of making other people happy."

"Tell you what, Kit," said Tom suddenly, taking his elbows off the sill—"I mean to ask the boys at our school to contribute."

CHAPTER IX.

TOM IS IN TOO MUCH OF A HURRY.

THE summer holidays began on the twenty-eighth of July. That day being also Miriam's birthday, she invited her two special friends round to a little picnic tea in the plantation. Great fun they had, too, for they packed their own basket, and wheeled it there on Miriam's garden barrow; they boiled their own kettle on a tripod over a fire of sticks which they had a great deal of trouble in lighting; and finally, they made their own tea and spread their own feast, and sat down on the grass to enjoy it.

Of course Katie was not invited. That was not to be expected, although in times past she had always been asked to Miriam's birthday picnics. But Katie's thoughts were otherwise occupied that glorious summer afternoon. The picnic party had just settled themselves to their fancy, when a sound of wheels and voices was heard along the road.

"Do let's run and look," cried restless little Terry

Grainger, the younger of the two friends, jumping up all in a hurry, and then glancing back at the feast, half doubtful about leaving it unless the others came too.

"No, don't let's," contradicted Madge Tewson, who was noted for wanting to fall to work whenever there was anything nice to be eaten. "We shall find our tea full of flies and spiders when we come back."

"Nonsense!" cried Miriam, who being hostess had the casting vote; and off she ran with Terry, leaving Madge to please herself about following.

"Well, I do declare!" exclaimed Miriam, tiptoeing to get her head above the palings.

Terry was at a disadvantage, not being so tall. "What is it, Mirry?" asked she eagerly, as she searched about for something to clamber on; "do tell!"

"The queerest caravan you ever saw!" replied Miriam. "The oddest little object in the shabbiest old bath-chair, with Tom and Katie pushing behind, and a common girl in her great-grandmother's clothes walking like a lady at the side."

Terry had surmounted her difficulties by this time, and even Madge Tewson, catching Miriam's words, had left the spread and joined them.

"Well, I *do* declare!" echoed Madge. "What next, I wonder? What on earth are Tom and Katie Rivers about?"

The plain fact of the matter was this: Katie's scheme had actually come to pass, and she and Tom had been to the station to meet their visitors and fetch them home.

Miriam was quite right. It *was* an odd-looking cavalcade. The bath-chair was an old one in which Mrs. Rivers's mother had ridden in and out to take the air, and since the day when her need of it had ceased, it had been Tom and Katie's chariot in the garden. Small wonder if it looked shabby.

In this chariot, however, sat Tab, supremely happy, and altogether unmindful that the leather was worn or the varnish scraped. To her the stuffed cushions, hard as they had grown with use, were luxury itself, and to ride was a queenly thing. All Tab knew was that she was actually in that unhoped-for paradise of loveliness and peace, *the country;* and that it far surpassed her brightest coloured dreams—for Tab had dreamt night and day of it ever since she first heard she was to go. There she sat, speechless with timidity and happiness, her little bundle resting on her thin, scantily-covered knees, and her hands tightly clasped upon it, in wonder and admiration. As for the rest, she was, to use Miriam's expression, "the oddest little creature" with her deformed, stunted body, and her big head, surmounted by its fantastic hat—the first she had ever worn—a sample of her own millinery, rigged up out of odd scraps from her second-hand dollies' finery.

Meanwhile by the side walked Zillah, "like a lady," not even carrying her own bundle, which had considerately been tucked away on the foot of the chair, so that her hands might be free to hold the wild flowers which London children often find it so difficult to realize are theirs to gather. But Zillah was not like poor little shy, misshapen Tab, who never saw a face, year in, year out, except Zillah's and her father's. She was sharp and quick, used to pushing her way about and bargaining with the second-hand venders, of whom she bought her stock-in-trade; and her delight, unlike Tab's, showed itself in excited chatter.

"Why, I know!" cried Terry Grainger: "that's what we overheard the girls talking about the day after Katie's hay-making party, you remember—about the city slum children."

"And they've actually fetched them here to make the country nasty too!" exclaimed Madge. "We shall have a fever breaking out in the place."

"I never thought they would actually do it," said Miriam, in a tone of contempt that seemed to betray a little annoyance at being out of it. "Fancy pushing them through the open streets too! I wonder, will Katie have them to sleep in her room?" she added ironically.

"Oh no," replied Terry, who was rather apt to take Miriam's sarcasms seriously; "they're to lodge at Mrs. Bull's. I heard Tiny Radford say so."

"Oh my!" cried Miriam; "what fun Dick Bull will make of that odd little creature's hump!"

The bath-chair was almost close under the fence just as Miriam said this, and Katie heard, if Tab did not—she hoped Tab did not hear. But Zillah's sharp ears had caught the words, and she had seen the jeering face that was peeping over the fence. She looked round at Katie with flushed cheeks. It had never struck her how much her poor afflicted sister might have to endure in exchange for her release from the imprisonment of that out-of-the-way garret where her deformity was hidden away.

Meanwhile Miriam had given the signal to return to the feast. "We shall have the rattlesnakes stealing our cakes, girls," said she, in a tone meant for the bath-chair party to hear; but the words had no sooner left her lips than she uttered a piercing scream of terror. In stepping back from the fence she had all but placed her foot upon an adder, and the creature was rearing up its head and hissing spitefully, just about to strike.

"Help, help!" screamed she. "It's going to kill me!" And Madge and Terry, joining in the scream, cried "Help, help!" too.

Tom heard their screams, and thought at first

they were pretending; but it soon became apparent that there was no make-belief about the matter, and letting go the handle of the bath-chair, Tom dashed across the road.

"What's the matter?" shouted he, as he sprang up the bank. Then seeing the enraged viper, he cleared the fence, and seizing a stout piece of wood which fortunately lay to hand, he aimed a desperate blow at the creature's backbone.

"Well done!" cried Tom triumphantly, repeating the blows with vigour to make sure of his work.

Miriam began to stammer out some thanks; but somehow Tom felt in no mood to listen to them after the rude manner in which she had spoken of poor Tab.

"I should advise you to clear out of here," said he, cutting her short and hurrying back to the fence.

But Tom, like the rest of us, was apt to make mistakes. He was in too much of a hurry, for he was not giving Miriam a fair chance; and he punished himself. In dashing over the fence he lost his balance and half fell; and his foot, finding no hold on the slippery grass bank, slipped down, throwing him forward on his face, and twisting his ankle terribly.

Tom had hard work not to cry out. He was obliged to sit down by the roadside to bear the pain. "The thing is," he said, " how I'm to get home."

Katie looked very serious. "It isn't *far*," suggested she hopefully.

"Too far to walk," said Tom pretty positively, screwing up his face with the pain, which was rapidly getting worse. "It's all that horrid Miriam's fault. I said I'd never help her again; but I forgot when I heard her scream. I wish I hadn't."

Ah, Tom! better far be governed by your generous impulses. Second thoughts are not *quite* always best, for they are often far more selfish. So Katie thought.

"O Tom!" she cried: "it wasn't Miriam's fault; and she'd be ever so sorry if she knew how you're hurt."

But Miriam was in entire ignorance of what had happened. Too much frightened to enjoy themselves any longer in the plantation, she and her friends had hurried off to remove their feast to the safer though more commonplace garden grass-plot.

Meanwhile it was hardly a suitable time to choose for discussing Miriam's disagreeable temper while Tom was in such pain. The most important consideration was how to get him home. After due conference the following plan was hit upon. Tab was to get out of the chair and sit by the roadside with Zillah, whilst Katie helped Tom in and wheeled him home; after which she would return at once and take Tab on to her destination.

CHAPTER X.

STRANDED HIGH AND DRY.

TAB and Zillah felt rather like fishes out of water, stranded high and dry upon their wayside bank, as Katie and the bath-chair disappeared round the turn of the road. Katie had started off at a brisk pace, promising not to be longer gone than she could possibly help; but the minutes seemed like hours.

Both children were very quiet at first. Tab looked about in a timid, constrained sort of way, wondering at the surpassing loveliness of the cool green canopy overhead, and the shadows of the trees upon the sunlit stretch of meadow-land beyond, and the blueness of the sky; listening to the twittering of the birds, and the distant sheep-bells, and the lowing of some patient cows in Mr. Grayson's yard, where they were waiting to be milked—sounds so different to those that reached her in the garret she called home. There she only heard the far-off, restless roar of traffic in the streets, and when that hushed to rest, the striking of the clocks that told her how the sleepless hours went. But here the very leaves seemed singing out for joy, and every happy insect in the air had music in its wings. This was the *country*, the beautiful country from which her father had returned each hay-making season she could remember, with money to pay for the things they owed, and perhaps to lay by for the rainy days—twice or thrice as much as the three of them could have earned in the time at home, where all the people round were starved for want of work. She had often tried to picture it, holding the money in her wasted hand, and listening to his talk about the fields and lanes where he had earned it; and one time he had even brought a coloured print to give her some idea of what " the country " was. But what was money and what was coloured print to all that her eyes saw now? It seemed like heaven itself. It took away her powers of speech.

Zillah, on the contrary, was silent because she dared not speak. She was used to jostling through the busy streets, and in this country lane there was not a single soul in sight. Something in the stillness almost frightened her. She looked nervously from side to side; saw flowers that she longed to pick, but dared not stir to reach them; noticed sparrows flitting in and out the boughs, just like the same brown birds that perched about the sooty

London chimney-pots at home; half wondered if they really were the *very* same, and whether they had followed Tab and her upon their holiday, but dared not tell her thoughts to Tab, for very fear of hearing her own voice. And so they sat, these two poor garret children on the grassy bank, waiting for Katie's return.

About ten minutes had passed in this manner, and Zillah's lively tongue was just on the point of breaking restraint, when who should come in sight but Dick Bull, driving his step-brother before him with a pair of reins. The sight of a live being unloosed Zillah's tongue at once.

"Look, Tab!" cried she, nudging her sister's elbow; but poor little Tab only shrank back behind her with a frightened look. She was unused to seeing and being seen.

Dick, intent upon his step-brother, did not perceive the two strange figures on the bank until he got right opposite. Then he pulled up short with the abrupt exclamation, "Hullo! who are you?"

Dick wouldn't have looked very terrible as *one* in a throng of people such as Zillah was accustomed to; but here, in this lonely lane, and face to face, he put the poor child's courage all to flight. She turned an appealing glance on her poor little elder sister.

Tab's white face had flushed crimson, not so much

with *fear* as because she was so entirely unused to seeing strangers. Before she could find an answer, Dick had snacked his reins and driven his horse up closer.

"Where in the world did you drop down from?" asked he.

"London," answered Tab, growing pale again.

"Might as well 'a' stopped there, for all I can see," said Dick rudely. "I should like to know what you came for."

"Because a lady wrote and asked us," said Tab. "We're to stay at a cottage somewhere here. Ah, it's *so* beautiful!" added Tab, half to herself.

"Beautiful, is it?" ejaculated Dick. "I tell you what, though—I believe you're the very gals what my mother's going to take in. Blest if I think she'd 'a' had you if she'd 'a' knowed what you was like. You're a rum-looking gal, you are!"

Tab coloured painfully. "I can't help it," said she simply.

"Didn't say you could," said Dick. "I say, though, that other one looks as if she'd make a smarter horse than this 'ere;" and Dick gave his reins a twitch that made his step-brother cry out, and rub his arm where the cord was tied.

"Who is he?" asked Tab, interested in the poor little fellow, on account of his miserable appearance.

"He's my horse," replied Dick, twitching the

reins again. "He wants the whip pretty often, too. His name's silly Tim; and he ain't quite right."

"That's a pity," said Tab sorrowfully. She had thought that in the country everybody must be happy.

Dick didn't vouchsafe an answer to this remark, for he was busy trying to unfasten the reins off Tim's arms.

"We'll see what sort of a horse that one makes," said he, nodding towards Zillah. "I'm going to drive her home. I'll bet *she* can run."

The cord had slipped into a knot, however; so after some few ineffectual attempts at undoing it, Dick got out his knife. But, fortunately for Zillah, at this very moment Katie reappeared with the bath-chair; and Zillah, springing to her feet, ran down the lane to meet her.

CHAPTER XI.

IN THE COUNTRY.

WHEN Zillah made her sudden escape Dick had shut his knife and gathered up Tim's reins, with a loud "Get up!" but he changed his mind, and pulled Tim up again, and stood there opposite Tab, staring at her.

"That's your sister, ain't it?" said he presently, following Zillah with his eyes.

Tab answered, "Yes."

"She ain't much like you," said Dick.

"She's straight, and I'm not," said Tab.

"I like you best, though," observed Dick, "straight or crooked. She runs away, and you don't."

"I *can't*," returned Tab gravely. Else perhaps she would have.

But by this time Katie had regained them with the bath-chair. Dick noticed that Zillah kept on the other side of the chair whilst Tab was being helped in, and he reflected, with satisfaction, that when she was at his mother's it would not always be possible to keep out of his hands so easily. Dick had made up his mind that he meant to have his pennyworth of fun out of Zillah. As soon as the others moved on he gave Tim the reins and moved on too, following slowly at a distance of a few paces.

Katie pointed up the drive as they passed the gate. "That's where our home is," said she, "but there's a good half-mile to go yet to where you are to stay."

Dick sprang forward. "I'll wheel 'em up for you, miss," said he, "and bring the chair back too."

There was something particularly obliging in the tone of Dick's voice; but Katie had no intention of yielding up her *protégées* to *his* tender mercies. She thanked him, and declined.

"It'll tire *you* awfully," Dick declared; "you ain't so strong as me, and it's all uphill after we get to the bottom here." But Katie still declined.

"Let me push, anyhow," begged Dick, anxious to get the matter into his own hand somehow or other. "Here!" added he, thrusting Tim's reins into Zillah's hands; "*you* drive *him*." Then laying hold of the chair, he commenced pushing so vigorously that it seemed to go like a feather.

Katie gave in, for, truth to tell, she was rather glad of the relief. She had hurried up the hill, and was a wee bit tired. But Dick pushed so fast that it didn't make things much better. When Katie remonstrated he only grinned, and said he " guessed they wanted their tea by now; and she wasn't bound to come with 'em except to please herself. He'd take 'em home all right enough." Katie viewed the matter differently, however, feeling bound to see them safely into Mrs. Bull's hands.

Meanwhile poor Tim was enjoying the novelty of a new hand on his reins. Zillah drove more gently, and was beginning to enter into the fun, as her strangeness wore off, " tchek-tcheking " to make him go. So Tim trotted briskly along by Tab's side, with his great unmeaning eyes fixed on her face, and a silly smile playing about his mouth. And Tab— whose kind heart had warmed to the poor half-witted boy because, like herself, he was different to other people—nodded pleasantly from time to time, and gave him back his smiles. In this way they arrived at Mrs. Bull's, where Katie, after introducing them to their temporary guardian, left them, and made the best of her way home to Tom.

Dick was right for once. Tab and Zillah *did* " want their tea;" and encouraged by kind Mrs. Bull's motherly care, a right good meal they made of it. Moreover, Tom and Katie's generosity had provided that this first " country " tea should be an extra tempting and substantial one; and for the first time in their lives they tasted new-laid eggs and green-gage jam and sweet dough cake.

Then their room, too—such a pretty little room! Its lattice window neatly curtained with white and clustered with sweet honeysuckle and the "seven sisters" rose. Its clean blue-patterned paper, too, hung with picture texts, and its bright-coloured bedside carpets in red and green squares. And the bed itself, so fresh and sweet and clean. Tab and Zillah had never in their lives seen anything like it before. How they slept that night, and how rested and refreshed they awoke, with the morning sunlight shining on their blind! It all seemed like one long, delightful dream, too lovely to be true.

Tom, on the contrary, hardly got a wink of sleep, his ankle was in such dreadful pain; and worse than that, his mind was very ill at ease, for he kept on wilfully blaming Miriam for what he knew to be no fault of hers—grudging the noble service that his chivalry had prompted him to do her.

Tom's chivalry was very far from perfect at present. He had yet to learn to serve friend and foe alike with willing love, as Christ his Master did upon the cross. But Tom didn't look at his knight-errantry in that light. He had meant never to help Miriam again since that day down by the pond, when she had refused his help so disagreeably; and then, after all, when his better self had forgotten that unchristian resolution in the impulse of the moment, he had not only spoilt his heroic action by refusing to listen to her thanks, and thus robbed Miriam of her chance of regaining her place in his and Katie's friendship, but had also, in his foolish hate, brought about his own punishment in the shape of all this suffering. But Tom only thought of Miriam's hateful temper, and wished he had let the adder sting her. "It would have served her right to lose her leg," said he to himself, "and I'll never, *never* help her out of a difficulty again."

Tom didn't say his prayers that night. He didn't want to; and it didn't seem like going to bed when night came, because he had been there ever since half-past five. Besides, he fancied that he couldn't say them with that constant throb in his ankle; so he didn't try. But Terry Grainger did, and added, "Bless Tom Rivers for jumping over the fence to kill the adder for us;" and God heard that little prayer, all in his own good time, and answered it, though not perhaps exactly in the way Tom would have chosen.

CHAPTER XII.

ALWAYS AFTER MISCHIEF.

KATIE walked over to Mrs. Bull's cottage next morning to see how Tab and Zillah were getting on, and also to take a little basket of gooseberries which she and Tom had been saving up on their own bushes for Tab and Zillah's special treat. Mrs. Bull was only paid, of course, to provide them with a bed and such plain fare as she would have given to her own two boys; but Tom and Katie wanted their guests to have a real good time, so they intended carrying them some little dainty every day. All this made it very vexing for Tom that he could not get about. But that was not to be thought of; so Katie set out alone, promising to be sure and explain that the yellow ones were off Tom's tree, and the red ones off her own—which was the best she could do towards mending matters.

Katie found Tab sitting on an old three-legged stool in the porch, with her lap full of flowers. Silly Tim had gathered them and brought them to her one by one. Dick had gone to carry home some mangling for his mother, and Tim was enjoying himself. He had taken quite a violent fancy to Tab. Something in her timid, gentle manner attracted the poor boy, who was so used to being hustled and driven.

Zillah, with the tabby kitten on her shoulder, was wandering up and down the narrow cinder-ash paths between the garden beds, wondering at the butterflies that country children take so little notice of. This tabby kitten was almost the only familiar object Zillah had come across; and it seemed to know that it had found a friend in her.

After talking to Tab for a few minutes, Katie went to fetch Zillah to the porch, and brought out her gooseberries, which she emptied into their laps, so that she might take her basket home. She had not long closed the garden gate when Dick returned with the empty clothes-basket.

"Hullo!" exclaimed he. "Gooseberries!"

"The young lady brought them," explained Zillah, who had quite recovered the use of her tongue since her night's rest.

"Ah!" said Dick.

"Won't you have some?" said Tab, timidly scooping up a handful out of her lap from among the flowers, and offering them to him.

Dick took them without scruple.

Presently Tim appeared round the corner of the house with a head of crimson sweet-william in his hand. Seeing Dick, he was drawing back out of sight; but Tab beckoned him. "I've got some gooseberries, Tim," cried she; "come and have some."

Tim still hesitated. But Tab still beckoned him with her shy, winning smile, holding out a fine red gooseberry—the finest she could see. Such an invitation was not to be refused. Tim came slowly forward, laid the flower on her lap with the rest, and took the gooseberry, which he put straight to his mouth. But that unlucky sweet-william had opened Dick's eyes. Seeing flowers in Tab's lap along with Katie's gooseberries, Dick had jumped to the conclusion that Katie had brought *them* too.

He guessed now where his mistake was.

"Who picked those flowers?" asked he roughly.

Tim shrank and cowered. He had only thought about giving Tab pleasure, because he liked her; but the tone of Dick's voice told him pretty sharply that he had done wrong. Poor Tim was always doing things like that—forgetting, out of sheer silliness, poor idiot that he was!

"Always after mischief!" cried Dick, cramming the gooseberries into his mouth two at a time, and holding out his hand for more.

"What business have you picking the flowers? I'll teach you—"

But Dick held out his hand in vain, for Tab had only three or four left, and Tim was to have those, she said.

"What!" cried Dick, "when he's been and got in mischief? Look here! Runners, and peas, and all! *I'll* teach him!" And Dick made such a terrible gesture that Tim fled for his life round the corner.

"He kept on bringing them to me," said Tab. "I didn't know he'd no business to. The young lady said we might pick any flowers we liked."

"Out of doors," said Dick—by which he meant in the hedges and ditches; "not in people's gardens, and *he* knows that well enough. Runners, and peas, and all!" repeated Dick indignantly; "the young *varmint!*"

"Runners and peas?" asked Zillah. "Which are they?"

Dick selected a specimen of each.

"They're good to eat," said he, "and he's been and picked 'em."

"*Flowers good to eat!*" Tab was surprised.

"Not the flowers, but the peas and beans," Zillah corrected her. Zillah had seen them on the costermongers' barrows, though she didn't know until then, any more than Tab did, that they grew from pretty flowers.

"*You* ha'n't picked any, I s'pose?" said Dick in a threatening tone, turning on Zillah. "You ha'n't given me any o' *your* gooseberries."

Zillah shook her head in answer to Dick's question, and tendered up a tribute of her precious fruit. She was naturally of a more greedy disposition than her sister, so it cost her a much keener pang to part with her gooseberries than it had Tab; but she was rather afraid of Dick.

"I ha'n't picked *one*," said she.

"So much the better for *you*," remarked Dick, as he munched the gooseberries. Then seeing that Zillah had prudently placed the remaining few out of reach of his covetousness by eating them herself, he added,—

"*Now* I'll go and teach Tim not to pick peas and beans again." And off he strode.

Tab gathered the few remaining gooseberries up out of her lap and put them in her pocket. Then she got up off the three-legged stool and looked uneasily at Zillah, and from Zillah towards the direction in which Dick had gone. It was in her mind to go and see what Dick was about to do to poor Tim. But Tab was not very strong on her legs, and she was so unused to walking abroad that she hardly knew how to set about it. Somehow it seemed so different to getting about the little garret at home.

Zillah opened her eyes on seeing the gooseberries disappear in Tab's pocket. "Ain't you going to eat 'em?" asked she. The child had a sort of idea that if they were eaten at all she would get her share, and that would partly make up for those she had been obliged to give up to Dick. But Tab shook her head. "I'm going to keep 'em for Tim," said she; so Zillah said no more about it.

"Where are you going, Tab?" asked she next, as Tab, after balancing herself a few moments, in order to get used to the new position of standing, stepped stiffly down on to the gravel.

"Going to look what Dick's after with Tim," was the reply; and Tab slowly made her way round the corner of the house, and down the cinder path between the rows of peas and beans, from which the unlucky flowers had been plucked.

"Never knew they growed like that afore," said Zillah to herself, as she followed. How should she, poor child?

But nothing was to be seen of either Dick or Tim, and Tab finally returned to the porch, very tired with her search. In the garden hedge was a gap through which Tim was in the habit of making his escape when he had incurred his brother's displeasure, and Dick had gone through after him.

CHAPTER XIII.

A WHITE LIE.

MRS. GRAYSON had been rather surprised to see the three children carting in their picnic tea from the plantation. But in giving the reason Miriam had not told the *whole* truth. She knew quite well that if her mother heard how Tom Rivers had come to the rescue, she would insist upon his being properly thanked, and Miriam was in no mood for humbling herself so far. She therefore simply said that they had seen an adder in the grass, and thought it wisest to come away at once—a piece of prudence which Mrs. Grayson heartily commended. The adventure, however, rather upset Miriam's enjoyment for the rest of the day, not only by frightening her, but because, try as she would to justify herself, conscience would not let her be quite comfortable about the half-truth she had told.

To be sure, it was not a downright *lie*. It was true they had come away because of the adder they had seen; but it was also true that Tom had risked himself for their sakes, and Miriam had an uncomfortable foreboding that some time or other, some *how* or other, that other half of the truth would come out. For truth is like a jack-in-the-box. The least touch undoes the catch that keeps it hidden; then back flies the lid and up pops its head, and the secret is out.

As it happened, it came out sooner than even Miriam expected.

Great-uncle Merry always came down to see them about this time, and as he could not come on Miriam's birthday, he had written to fix the day after. Miriam was a good deal excited about it. He had sent her a lovely scrap-album, for which she wanted to thank him; she was also very anxious to show off the gold locket which she had bought with his half-sovereign, and to coax the old gentleman into allowing her to take one of his silver ringlets to fix inside the glass opposite his portrait. But by the time Uncle Merry arrived a cloud had drifted up into Miriam's sky.

Mrs. Grayson, walking up to the shops, to see if she could procure some asparagus—of which Uncle Merry was particularly fond—had met Tom and Katie's mother, and learned the whole history of the adventure with the adder.

After dinner Uncle Merry proposed a walk.

Mrs. Grayson always rested of an afternoon. Not

being over strong, her morning's household duties tired her. But Uncle Merry, despite his seventy and odd years, was always ready for a stroll as soon as he had smoked his pipe; and he was quite content to see his niece comfortably settled on the couch whilst Miriam accompanied him.

"Trust us for getting along all right together; hey, Mirry?" said the old gentleman, reaching out his hand to catch hers; for they always went about hand-in-hand. "We'll just have a look at the poultry-yard, and smell the hay; then we'll stroll down to the plantation and round the field, and by the time we get back you'll be waking up for tea."

Mrs. Grayson smiled and nodded as she settled herself among the sofa cushions. "I should advise you, though, to be careful how you go in the plantation, uncle," said she. "Adders have found their way there."

"Adders, eh!" exclaimed Uncle Merry. "That's a pity. It's such a pretty place to stroll in. Londoners like me think a world of trees and greenery after all the bricks and chimney-pots. We ought to put a premium of half-a-crown apiece on their heads—like one of our English kings did upon the wolves—and get the place cleared of the pest. But we'll take care; so don't be fidgety on our account, and spoil your nap."

Mrs. Grayson promised, saying she wasn't afraid

to trust Uncle Merry to be prudent; so he and Miriam went off together.

At the first mention of adders Miriam had hung her head and begun to feel uncomfortable. She didn't exactly want that Uncle Merry should hear the whole of the story. But Miriam's mamma was not one to tell tales; and as for Uncle Merry, he was so much taken up with all there was to be seen directly they got outside, that he asked no further questions about the plantation. He went round and looked at all the sitting-hens in their wicker coops on the lawn, and heard how many there were in each brood, and how each mother-bird declined to allow members of her neighbours' families to intrude under her wings. He watched old Spinks milking the cows, and asked him no end of questions about the hay and other crops, and went to smell the fresh, sweet stacks; for Uncle Merry, like all Londoners, was very fond of hay, and would have romped like any tomboy if he had come down whilst it was being tossed. Then he walked on through the orchard and down the field to the gate of the plantation.

"We must peep over, even if we don't go in," said Uncle Merry, resting on the gate. Then he began to ask about the adders—how many had been seen, and who had seen them, and so forth.

Miriam told him "only one," and that it had been

killed; and by degrees it all came out how she and Madge and Terry were going to have tea there, out among the trees, when they were frightened away by this horrid viper; but how a boy, hearing their screams, had jumped over the fence and beaten it to death with a stick.

Miriam was rather fond of relating adventures, and she had unconsciously pictured the incident so graphically that Uncle Merry listened with breathless interest. The only detail she kept back was the name of the hero; but that didn't suit Uncle Merry.

"Well," observed he, "all's well that ends well. But you haven't told me your deliverer's name. He was a plucky chap, and he deserves a gold medal."

Miriam answered that he was brother to a schoolfellow of hers.

"I should think his sister must be proud of him," said Uncle Merry.

Miriam held her tongue. All her sprightliness seemed to have vanished on a sudden.

"Yes," resumed Uncle Merry, "he richly deserves a gold medal, this—what's his name?"

"Tom," said Miriam reluctantly.

"This Tom," repeated Uncle Merry. "But after all," continued he, "I'd give more for a lad whose brave deeds weren't done for the sake of any medal.

The knights in olden times, you know, were quite content to have the lady's thanks; and I daresay this Tom was quite content with yours. You'll be grand friends, you and Tom."

Miriam still held her tongue.

"I should like to thank him too," said Uncle Merry. "I feel as if I owed him a good deal for his defence of my grandniece—a good deal more than any medal could repay."

This was getting too hot for Miriam. "Very likely he wouldn't want your thanks," said she, looking down and plucking at the leaves on the hedge. Miriam was very uncomfortable, and heartily wished her temper hadn't got her into such a hobble.

"Not want my thanks!" exclaimed Uncle Merry in surprise. "Why? I should have thought he would have been just a trifle proud of himself. Heroes usually like to wear their laurels."

"He wouldn't have *my* thanks," said Miriam, a trifle sullenly.

"Ah! of course he's modest," said Uncle Merry, "and pretends he hasn't done anything worth making so much fuss about. But I've a very great mind," added Uncle Merry, "to give him a gold medal just because he *is* a modest boy and a brave one too. What do you say to that?" He brought a gold sovereign out of his waistcoat pocket. "He deserves every farthing of that."

"No he doesn't," cried Miriam, with sudden determination; "and he isn't modest at all. He's a nasty, disagreeable boy, and I hate him, Uncle Merry."

Uncle Merry had never looked so utterly astonished in his life, or at least Miriam had never seen him look so. "Hate the boy that saved your life!" cried he. "Never!"

Then Miriam was obliged, in self-justification, to tell the whole story over, from the first day in the plantation, when Tom behaved so badly about the primroses, to the day of her ill-fated picnic-party, when he sprained his ankle in his ill-natured haste to get away from her.

"Here's a kettle of fish!" exclaimed Uncle Merry when he had heard it all. "Tom doesn't deserve his gold medal so thoroughly as I thought."

"He don't deserve it at all," interrupted Miriam, who felt rather like crying by this time.

"And I'll tell you what," said Uncle Merry, looking grave: "no more did you deserve that gold half-sovereign you bought the locket with; for you are as bad as Tom, and there's a pair of you."

Miriam's countenance fell further still.

"Yes," said Uncle Merry, "it's six of one and half-a-dozen of the other; and I don't see a pin to choose between you."

"But it's all Tom's fault," reasoned Miriam; "he began it by teasing me."

"Very bad of him, too," returned Uncle Merry. "But if little girls don't learn to take teasing good-humouredly, they'll grow up dreadful-tempered women. If you had given Tom good-natured answers, you'd have turned all his gibes and jeers into fun—which is what you boys and girls are all so fond of.

"Now I'll tell you what I'd like to see both you and Tom do," continued Uncle Merry, as Miriam bit her lips and looked down. "I'd like to see you join a band of kindness—not pledged to look out for heroic deeds to do, you know; but just to do the little, simple acts of daily kindness that go to make life sweet. Heroic deeds are like birthdays and anniversaries, and the grottoes poor children build with oyster-shells and bits of tile—'they're only once a year.' It would be a terrible world if there were adders to kill and giants to slay every day of the year. But little acts of kindness are to be done every day, and every minute of the day; and by doing them we get our hands in for the greater acts."

But it was now time to return to the house for tea; so Uncle Merry took his arms off the gate, and they began to retrace their steps. But Miriam no longer laughed and chatted gaily, as she had done coming out, for she could feel that she had lowered herself in Uncle Merry's eyes.

"Now when I'm gone," said Uncle Merry, as they crossed the lawn towards Mrs. Grayson, who was stepping out to meet them, "think what there is that you could do to make Tom's time pass pleasantly. Take him a book to read, or gather him a bunch of flowers, or get your scissors and cut him a basketful of that lovely mustard and cress that is to burn my mouth at tea; and let him see that you are sorry for the accident he met with in serving you, and that you are ready to go halfway towards making the quarrel up."

And Miriam had more than half a mind to do it.

CHAPTER XIV.

PULLING ONIONS.

WHILST Great-uncle Merry was leaning on the plantation gate lecturing Miriam, Tom was grumbling away in style upon his couch, with the injured ankle on a cushion; and whilst Katie was doing her best to console and amuse Tom, Tab in turn, after her own quaint fashion, was lecturing Dick.

When last we heard of Dick he had gone through the hole in the hedge after silly Tim. Now Dick never went on this quest after his unfortunate stepbrother but. he returned triumphant; for Tim's utmost cunning consisted in skulking a little way along the lane beyond the field, and squatting down to hide behind a gate-post or tree-trunk. The consequence was that Tim came in to dinner blubbering miserably to himself; and when Tab held open her pocket-slit to show him the gooseberries, he cast a frightened look towards Dick, and actually ran away.

Tab guessed all about it in a minute. Dick, determined that Tim should not have the gooseberries she had refused to him, had taken means to convince the poor fellow that it would be better not to defy his wishes. But this time Dick had gone a little *too* far. Just as Tim ran out in came the father, tired with his long morning's work, and hungry for his dinner. Now Dick's father was not a mild man, and if the boys were not in the kitchen ready to sit down as he set foot on the threshold, he invariably kicked up a fuss.

"Where be Tim?" snarled he, casting his eye round.

"Just this very minute run out again," responded Mrs. Bull, as she lifted the saucepan to turn out the dish of rice and skimmed milk with which the children were to commence. "Dick had better go and fetch him in."

However, Dick returned to say that Tim was nowhere about. The fact was, he had taken flight through the gap in the hedge again; and it did not suit Dick's purpose to follow him up just as dinner was being served out. But Tim's father was not satisfied. He had more than once had to administer correction in Tim's defence.

"Tell you what!" exclaimed he, bringing his fist down on the table with such force that Tab and Zillah burned their mouths with the hot rice,—" tell you what it is! You've been at him again. Now you've got to fetch him in before you have a bit of dinner." And Dick knew by past experience that there was no appeal; so out he rushed, bent upon hunting Tim in pretty quickly.

When Dick's father had disposed of his bacon and greens, and finished his crust of bread and cheese, he pushed back his chair, and looked so terrible at Dick that Tab and Zillah wondered what was coming. Dick, however, went on unconsciously enough, spooning away as fast as he could at his plate of rice, and after a minute or so Mr. Bull tipped his chair back on its hind legs and reached down a short clay pipe off the cupboard by the chimney-place. This he filled and lighted, after which he stood up from his chair and looked at Dick again. Then he walked to the door.

"Them two rows o' 'taters wants hoeing," said he, facing about again upon the threshold; "and them *injuns* must be pulled to-day. I want the bed broke up; and I shall look to see 'em laid to dry 'gin I come in again."

"A precious nice job with the sun right on your back!" grumbled Dick. "They can wait."

"Them as works with the sun on their backs ha'n't got no time for mischief," said Dick's father sternly. "Mind they're done, out of hand, afore I'm back, or you'll get ne'er a crumb this side o' to-morrow morning. Holidays don't do some people no good, but only makes 'em lazy and spiteful and good for nothing."

So all that afternoon, with the scorching August sun upon his back, and the perspiration beading on his brow, Dick had to work away at his penance.

By-and-by, when the shadow from the pear-tree lengthened, Tab left her seat in the porch and slowly made her way down the cinder-ash path between the beans and peas to where Dick was hoeing. Dick went on without looking up, and Tab stood watching, whilst the hoe chopped up the mould and gathered it together in a ridge along the row.

"What's that for?" asked she presently.

"To make anybody sweat, I should say," returned Dick promptly, unbending his back and pushing back his hat.

"What good does it do the plants, I mean?" said Tab.

"Makes 'em grow big 'taters," answered Dick.

Tab could not see any at present, and she said so, causing Dick to roar with merriment. "As if 'taters came like apples!" grinned he.

Tab inquired, "How then?" and was surprised to hear that they grew and multiplied beneath the soil from the slices of original potato that were planted there. These simple facts that Dick thought he never had to learn appeared such marvels to this poor child of brick-and-mortar London, who had never seen a green thing spring up in her life. "I should like making 'em grow," said she. "It'd seem that they must *love* me for it, like our sparrows do when Zill and me puts crumbs out on the tiles."

Such poetic fancy was beyond Dick's comprehension. "There's all them *injuns* yet to pull," returned he, thinking more about the hot sun on his back.

"Wish I could help you," Tab said shyly.

"*You* ain't good for pulling injuns," said Dick, with some contempt.

"Zill is, though," said Tab, looking round for her.

"Zill don't care for work," said Dick; "she'd rather be my horse, if I don't drive too hard."

"She works at home," said Tab. "Zill's a rare good girl," she added proudly.

"I'd rather bet on you nor her," said Dick.

"I think," said Tab presently, "that I could pull some 'injuns' if you showed me how." So Dick put down his hoe and came to show her how; and whilst Zillah frisked about after the butterflies in the field whither she had followed Tim through the gap, Tab's poor weak back was bent over the onion-bed against a row of scarlet-runners all in bloom. In a very little while she sat down on the cinder-path and pulled them so, because it tired her to stoop.

After a bit Dick, having got through with his hoeing, came and commenced pulling on the opposite side of the bed.

"It don't half make *you* hot," said Dick, whose own face was streaming by this time.

"I ha'n't been hoeing," answered Tab. "Besides, I like to feel the sun warm on my back. It never shines in our garret—only up on the roof, and bakes us, like an oven."

Dick pulled away in silence. He rather liked talking to Tab; only he was a bad hand at finding much to say.

"Tim's your brother, ain't he?" Tab asked suddenly, when they had been some while without speaking.

"Step-brother," corrected Dick.

"That don't make much difference, does it?" said Tab.

"His mother ain't *my* mother; that's all," explained Dick.

"She's good to you, though," said Tab; "and you're real bad to Tim. If I was you I'd be more kind to him, poor fellow."

Dick held his tongue, and Tab on her side said no more. But when the father came from work, and growled because all the onions weren't all pulled, she interposed. "He's gone on hard all the time," said she; "and I've been helpin' him."

CHAPTER XV.

TOM'S GOLD MEDAL.

FROM that day forward an odd kind of friendship sprang up between Tab and Dick, and it was very curious to watch the pains which the rough, rude boy would take to please her: how he would stand for an hour at a time against the porch trying to answer her many questions about the hundred and one things in country life that she was ignorant of; how he would catch moths and butterflies and beetles and caterpillars for her to look at, or instruct her in the mysteries of sowing and of gathering in—that "seed-time and harvest" of which till then poor Tab had known so little. But never again did he claim a share of Tab's good things, though perhaps he got no less on that account; and all this while poor silly Tim had peace.

Meanwhile, an important change had come over the appearance of the two slum children. Their poor old dust-coloured garments had given place to clean, bright prints—last year's frocks, which Mrs. Rivers had brought out and made over with Katie's help, sitting by Tom's sofa, near the open window.

"They look like butterflies just out of the chrysalis," Katie reported, after witnessing the metamorphosis.

They were fitted up with a stout new pair of boots each, too, and two cast-off hats of Katie's, which, if rather sunburnt as Katie's standard went, looked very neat and smart against the tawdry, faded head-gear in which they had left home. Better still, their thin arms grew daily plumper and more round with care and rest and better feeding; their wan, pale cheeks took on a healthy bronze out in the sunshine and free air from morn till night; and they lost the old, pinched look that London children have. Only now and again Tab, watching Zillah romping in the field with Tim, would heave a sigh to think that she must go back to her hard, dark life among the tiles. She did not mind so much about herself, for she could never dance with glee as Zillah did; so perhaps it didn't matter quite so much, she thought, that she should leave the sunshine and the flowers and go back to want and pinch. She did not even know that there is much want and pinch, too, even in the country, and that when the trees are bare and the heavens black, frost kills the birds among the boughs as well as underneath the city eaves. She only knew the country in the summer-time, and that was very beautiful.

Tab loved the birds, especially the blackbirds that awoke her with their sunrise hymns. Dick found that out, and promised he would catch her one to take back home. But Tab begged mercy for the little things. She could not bear to think of caging them as she was caged, when they had wings to fly. "God would be angry with me, I think," she told Dick in her simple way. Nevertheless, she was very pleased when he announced that he had found a nest to show her, and even trusted him to ride her down the field in the big wheelbarrow.

A week before, Dick would have plucked this nest ruthlessly from its bough, and laughed at the idea of caring for the anguish of the parent birds; but since Tab thought it cruel, the pleasure of it seemed gone.

All this while Tom and Katie were of course not Tab and Zillah's only benefactors. Most of the boys and girls who had contributed to afford them this holiday, felt bound to come and see them at the cottage; and almost each one brought some trifling gift. Some brought flowers, some nice things to eat. One, who had heard a good deal of talk about window-gardening for the London poor, collected a packet of seeds for Tab to sow when spring came round again; another brought some snowdrop bulbs and crocuses. Some sought out old toys and puzzles; others, left-off gloves and scarves. One girl had knitted woollen stockings for the winter-time; one had darned up several worn pairs of her own. One gave a crochet shawl that she was working for herself; another begged her mother's list, and made some nice warm stays: and so the presents kept on pouring in till Tab and Zillah felt themselves to be quite rich.

Miriam heard all about it from time to time through Terry Grainger, whose cousin, Tiny Radford, it was who had made the list stays. Tiny had tried hard to coax Terry into going with her to the cottage; but Terry was in too much fear of Miriam to venture upon such a step, and Madge Tewson, who was by, quite ridiculed the idea.

"As if they were princesses!" exclaimed she, "instead of nasty-smelling children from the slums, with ragged clothes and dirty faces. I should think they must be pretty well puffed up with self-conceit by this time. Half the people in the place have been to kiss their hands!"

"If you could see the difference in them since they came," argued Tiny, "I'm sure you'd wish that you were in it."

Now being "out of it" was just what aggravated

Miriam, only she would not have this known for anything.

"You talk as if there was nothing in the world to do but heap one's charity on their two heads," said she disdainfully; "as if there were no other poor!"

"Oh, I *know* there are," said Tiny—"so *very* many, quite as poor as they."

"Well, we've got our own scheme," said Miriam curtly, turning away and pulling Terry with her; "and we shan't ask *you* to help." And Miriam did think, just for the time, that she would give a children's Christmas dinner, or do something of the kind, when winter came. "I've only got to ask Great-uncle Merry," said she, quite confident that he would empty his purse into her lap when he heard of the scheme, and buy her all the usual presents besides. "Uncle Merry's very rich."

Meanwhile, Uncle Merry's injunction with regard to Tom had been entirely neglected, and poor Tom got out again and swung himself about on crutches without having received a word of thanks from her. Great-uncle Merry had not forgotten, though; and Tom had received the gold medal he had spoken of to Miriam, together with a letter full of thanks, begging its acceptance in token of his appreciation of the boy's heroic act.

Tom had never in his life before possessed a

sovereign all his own. To Katie it seemed a mine of money in itself. "You won't know what to do with it," said she.

"Oh, shan't I?" contradicted Tom. "Money soon slips through your hands. I want that model engine, and a box of compasses, and lots of things. I mean to be an engineer, you know, and build bridges and lay railways where even Stanley hasn't been. And perhaps I'll buy you something out of it."

Katie said nothing just then; but when the end of Tab and Zillah's stay drew near, she went and joined him one morning on the grass, where he lay reading in the shade of the wych-elm. "Tom," said she, "I wish that sovereign was mine."

"That you do, I'll wager," answered Tom. "Girls are always after money. What would you do with it?"

"Give Tab and Zillah just another week," said Katie, half in hopes that he would take the hint.

"That's more than either of them can expect," said Tom decidedly. "We can't give all our money up to them."

"O Tom," cried Katie, "I can't bear the thought of letting them go back."

"It's Miriam's turn," said Tom. "It isn't fair that we should do it all."

"Not fair, exactly, perhaps," said Katie thoughtfully. "That isn't what we've got to think about in doing good. We ought to do it just because we want to."

"And if we *don't* want to, we ought not," reasoned Tom, with false logic. "So there's an end of it;" and Katie said no more.

That afternoon Katie stole up to her room and took out her gold locket—the one she had worn at the party in the spring, when Miriam so envied her. It was a pretty one, and Katie's fingers lingered over it as she hung it round her neck. Then she took it off again, and turned it over many times, and finally she clasped it on again. Now it was not like Katie to be fond of dressing up, and just now she was only testing her powers of self-denial. She wanted to make sure that she would not be very sorry when it was too late to draw back.

Now it happened that Dick had taken it into his head to give Tab a great treat that afternoon. His father's master having bought a crop of pears in an orchard half-a-mile beyond, Dick had offered Tab the ride there in the barrow to see them gathered, and pick the bruised ones up; and Katie, standing near her window making up her mind, saw them all pass by—Tab in the barrow on a sack of straw, with Tim and Zillah harnessed on in front, and Dick to wheel behind, and all so full of fun and merriment that in an instant the scale was turned, and Katie's mind made up.

CHAPTER XVI.

A SAD LOSS.

THE question was, how to dispose of the locket, and how much it would fetch.

The jeweller and watchmaker in the street would buy it, Katie felt quite certain; but there was an uncomfortable doubt in her mind as to whether she had any right to part with it without her mother's leave. "It's my own," she reasoned; "and what is the use of having property of one's own, if one may not do as one pleases with it? It is not as if I wanted the price of it for a silly purpose. It is for such a good cause. Jesus said, 'Sell what thou hast, and give to the poor.' Surely mamma could not object."

"Then why not ask her?" said another voice, which Katie could not exactly answer. Just in the midst of her perplexity Mrs. Rivers called to her.

"Katie," said she, "here are some letters I want you to carry to the post; and you may take this pot of currant jelly round to Mrs. Bull's for Tab and Zillah. I have quite as much as I shall want without it; and their stay is nearly up."

There was an opportunity to broach the question of giving them another week; but there was also the chance of getting out alone and ascertaining for herself how much her generosity would bring her in, for the jeweller's was next door to the post-office. Quickly unfastening the locket from her neck and slipping it in her pocket, Katie put on her hat, and taking a pair of gloves out of her drawer, ran downstairs, putting them on as she went.

"There is no time to lose," her mother warned her as she held the letters out. "Post these first, and then go on to the cottage. You will be back in plenty of time for tea." So, with the letters and the basket in her hand, off ran Katie, feeling rather guilty, though, it must be owned.

There was no one in the jeweller's as Katie passed; so, quickly counting her letters and slipping them in the box, with a glance at the post-office clock to see they were in time, she turned back and stepped in.

The old jeweller was behind the counter, busy cleaning up his jewellery. "What can I show you, missie?" asked he, holding up the bit of silver filigree that he was brushing. "That's a pretty little brooch to send to anybody on their birthday," said he, turning it about so as to make the light glitter on it. Katie had more than once bought birthday gifts there for her little friends, and he thought she might be wanting one. But Katie shook her head.

"No thank you, Mr. Brett," said she. "I've no money to spend on birthdays just at present."

"Insolvent, eh?" laughed Mr. Brett, brushing away at the little brooch, which he held by its pin between the blackened tips of his finger and thumb. "All gone in sweets?"

Katie smiled; but she was too eager to proceed to business to make answer back. Her hand was already in her pocket. "I wanted you to tell me how much you could give me for this," she said with heightening colour, drawing out the locket and chain.

"How much?" repeated Mr. Brett, looking at her outstretched hand in some astonishment. "Why, you don't want to sell your locket?"

"I'm thinking about doing so," said Katie positively.

"But little girls that live at home don't need to sell their jewellery," objected Mr. Brett. "Their parents buy them all they want."

"I want to raise some money," said Katie, in a tone that rather seemed to say, "What for, is no concern of yours." "How much is it worth?" she asked again.

Mr. Brett took the trinket, turned it over, examined the carat mark, and weighed it in his hand. Then he pushed his glasses up and looked her in the eyes. "I know just what it's worth," said he, "because your father chose it from this very case my hand is on. But if I were to give you money for it, don't you see, I should be hauled over the coals for it, because you're not of age, and infants aren't allowed to sell their property? It isn't theirs, you know, because they're not their own. They belong to their parents, every bit of 'em, until they're twenty-one. So you must just go home, and if you're bent on parting with it, bring your parents' writing to the bargain. I couldn't buy it any other way."

Katie's face clouded over.

"If I were you," said Mr. Brett, "I'd give up such a ramshackle idea. Not every little lady of your age has such a handsome locket of her own."

"But then, you see, you don't know what it's for," said Katie, as she took the locket back. "It's not for anything that's wrong or silly, Mr. Brett; indeed it isn't," she added, lingering half in hopes he would relent.

"Of course not," answered Mr. Brett. "But that being so, why not take mamma into council on the subject?"

Katie left the shop disappointed, and turned her steps towards Mrs. Bull's.

Of course Tab and Zillah were not at home to thank her; Mrs. Bull took the opportunity of speaking a word in praise of them. "Two nice little girls as ever I'd wish to have under my roof, miss," said she, "'specially the afflicted one. And handy! I never saw a woman more quick in putting herself forward to help. Many's the time she's stirred the rice for me whilst I frizzled the bacon for my husband; and as to peeling the potatoes, I might say I ha'n't handled one since she's been here. She never once forgets a thing you tell her, either, like so many gals. As to Dick, he don't know how to make enough of her. It's just as if she'd tamed him, miss—made a lamb out of a wolf, as you might say. And yet he made such fun of her the first night she were here. I thought the poor little body'd never get a moment's peace. His father said to me when Dick were gone to bed, 'Look 'ere,' ses he: 'if Dick can't be considerate to them as is misfortunate, why, he'll get a taste o' strap, that's all.' But bless you! Dick ha'n't needed it; and he's let Tim alone the whole time through, and hardly teased him once."

"And they've got to go home on Monday," said Katie ruefully.

"It do seem a pity," said kind-hearted Mrs. Bull.

"I do declare I'll ask my old man if we can't give 'em a couple o' days more out of our own pocket. The parson preaches to us of the duty of giving to the heathen far away in distant lands; but *I* say, 'Charity begins at home.' Anyhow, 'twould be a downright pleasure, and we'd *see* what good we're doin' *them.*"

Katie went home wishing more than ever that she could find the money that she wanted. "O Tom!" cried she, kneeling on the grass beside him, and beating down a worm-cast with the handle of his crutch. "It's all no use. He wouldn't take it; and they'll have to go."

"Who wouldn't? Take what? Go where?" queried Tom.

"Oh, I forgot you didn't know," said Katie, colouring. "I didn't mean any one to know. I wanted Mr. Brett to give me money for my locket, to pay for Tab and Zillah's staying here another week."

"You little idiot!" cried Tom, with more force than politeness. "A good job that he didn't; you'd have caught it awfully."

"But, you see, I shall never care for it again," said Katie. "It's *pretty*; but of what real use are pretty things?"

"You're not an atom like a girl," said Tom, right puzzled. "Girls generally hanker after finery."

"I shouldn't care for anything, if only Tab and Zill could have another week," said Katie sadly.

Tom was silent, looking at his book. Suddenly he stretched his hand out. "Let's see what the locket's worth," said he. "Perhaps I'll lend you something on it. I shan't want *all* my sovereign yet awhile."

"O Tom, *will* you?" Katie cried. "I'll save up every farthing that I get, and pay you by degrees. You dear old Tom!"

"Of course," said Tom. "Let's look."

But Katie's face was blank with consternation and dismay. Her hand was in her pocket, and she felt and felt in vain.

"O Tom!" she cried, "what *shall* I do? It's gone. My locket's gone!"

CHAPTER XVII.

A LETTER TO BERMONDSEY.

A HOLE at the bottom of the pocket was the cause of this sad loss. Katie turned her pocket inside out, and sat upon the grass with her finger through the hole, gazing ruefully upon its emptiness.

Tom was the first to speak. "It's gone," said he; "that's certain. Clean gone!"

"What shall I do?" moaned Katie.

"All comes of being like a boy," said Tom consolingly. "I daresay that old knife of mine has worn the hole."

"What *shall* I do?" repeated Katie.

"Go and look for it, first thing," said Tom. "Perhaps you'll find it if you go along the road you came. I'd go at once, if I were you."

"Do you think there's any chance?" cried Katie, springing to her feet.

"Might be," said Tom. "At any rate, you needn't set up a howl until you've looked." So off went Katie, with her whole heart in her eyes, and searched every step of the way to Mr. Brett's, and back again to Mr. Bull's, even up the garden-path and into the front sitting-room, where she had stood to take the currant jelly out. But no locket was to be seen. Katie was well-nigh in despair.

"You'll make it public, won't you, miss," said Mrs. Bull, "and offer a reward?"

But the very thought of it made Katie hot. What would her parents say? It was a very heavy heart she carried home with her; for she had meant to do well, and just because she had been bent on doing it all alone, she had done very, very ill.

Tom guessed at a glance that her search had been in vain. "Well, that's a pretty go!" said he.

"I must go and tell mamma," said Katie, who had not the least thought in the world of hiding what she had done.

Tom said nothing; but he felt as if he would rather eat his own head than have such a terrible confession to make.

Mrs. Rivers was still writing in the dining-room when Katie went in. "Well, were my letters in good time?" she asked, as Katie came towards her. "I had meant this one to go also," she went on as Katie told her "Yes." "But the evening post will do. It is for Tab and Zillah's father. Guess what

I have written, Katie; I know you will be pleased."

It could be only *one* thing, Katie knew; but she positively could not find a word to say, she was so full of her own trouble.

"Why, how you've hurried!" her mother said, perceiving something was amiss. "You're quite out of breath, and in such a heat."

But Katie went straight to the point at once.

"O mother!" she cried, "I've been so naughty, and I meant to be so good;" and thereupon the whole history came out.

Mrs. Rivers looked serious, but she did not scold. "You intended to do well, dear; so you mustn't grieve. But it *was* a pity that you didn't ask me first, for you see I'd thought of doing the very thing you wanted."

Katie burst into tears. "I wanted the money to be my *very* own," said she, between her sobs. "And now I've lost the locket you and papa gave me, and done no good."

"Never mind," her mother told her soothingly. "The best-intentioned of us make mistakes, even your papa and I sometimes; and you will be the only sufferer, since Tab and Zillah are to have the extra week just the same. So dry your eyes, and after tea we will go round and take them their good news."

CHAPTER XVIII.

MIRIAM'S WISH.

NOTHING further was heard of the locket.

Mr. Rivers reported the loss at the police-station, and offered a reward; and Katie and her mamma made numerous inquiries in the neighbourhood, in hopes that some of the cottagers' children might have lighted on it, playing up and down. But all to no effect; and by the time that Tab and Zillah's extra week drew to a close, Katie had given up all hope of ever seeing it again.

Zillah cried at the prospect of leaving her happy dream behind. Tab did not cry. She thought less about herself. But she looked at Zillah with something like a mother's love, wishing—oh, so ardently—that she could stay back there, among the flowers and the butterflies. Only she would have hardly liked to trust her all alone; for Zillah was so fond of pretty things and frolicking, and Tab knew well that honest girls must work.

"She'd make a tidy servant, now, if she was

taught," said Mrs. Bull, as Tab sat talking whilst she ironed up the clothes that she had washed for them to take home clean. "Perhaps another year we might get her some light place hereabouts, where she'd be learning under my eye."

Tab looked eager. "I wish we could," said she. "Would anybody really take her, do you think?"

"Why not?" said Mrs. Bull. "She's strong-looking and well-grown, despite her many hardships; and many ladies, such as haven't got enough to fill their time, will take a girl like her to train and make a servant of. But you'd be lonesome, like; for you ain't strong enough to take a place."

Tab shook her head. "That wouldn't matter much," said she, "as long as I saw Zillah right. That's all I want; and then I'll pray Almighty God to take me where the angels are. I think I know just what it's like since I've been here." Just like that peaceful country place, the poor child thought, only lovelier and more peaceful, if that could be; God its light, and angels, with their golden harps and silver wings, instead of birds. That was Tab's idea of heaven; and she was content to wait till God should call her there, provided only Zill grew good and happy.

To Dick she said, "Now, when I'm gone you *will* be kind to Tim; now won't you, for my sake?"

"He'll have to be my horse again," said Dick. For Zillah had taken poor Tim's place the most part of the time, and Dick had found her much more fleet.

"You won't be cruel, and drive hard," Tab pleaded, with her hand upon his sleeve.

"P'raps; p'raps not," said Dick.

"But he's so silly and so weak—like me," said Tab. "He can't go fast like Zill. God made him so. You will be kind to him."

It was two o'clock when she and Zillah started home. Mrs. Rivers went with them to see them safe into their father's hands. She had chosen afternoon, so that they might have a good dinner first, and they took a large bundle of warm things for the winter with them, besides fresh butter, tea and sugar, new-laid eggs, a piece of bacon ready cooked, and other sundries, packed together in a hamper with the roots and seeds, and a great big posy of fresh-cut flowers on the lid. Zillah carried a large bunch of turnips and onions which Dick's father had given her; and Tab hugged in her arms a pumpkin marrow Dick had begged for her, to hang till winter-time. And so they took their places in the train, and waved farewell to all their many little benefactors, who had flocked to see them off.

Miriam and Madge Tewson met them going back.

Miriam tossed her head, and looked the other way; but Madge stood still and counted them aloud. "Three-and-twenty, I do declare!" exclaimed she in a mocking tone; "all to see the little ragamuffins off. Well, I hope they haven't left the plague behind."

"If they have, I hope that Tom and Katie Rivers may be the first to catch it," said Miriam.

"I call that downright wicked," said a boy who was walking between Katie and his sister.

"Wishes do come true sometimes," added the sister in a serious voice.

"Nonsense!" said Katie, who had been taught to laugh at superstitious notions. "I'm not afraid. It's a pity, though, that Miriam will say such things, when she might be friends all round;" and she nodded "Good-bye."

"Say, Kit!" broke out Tom, as they sat at tea—Katie pouring out in Mrs. Rivers's stead—"*what a jolly thing it is for Miriam's brother that she hasn't got one!*"

Katie laughed, and told him not to talk such Irish.

"But it just occurred to me," continued Tom, "what a cat-and-dog life they would lead."

Katie moved her spoon round slowly in her cup, and did not answer. She was thinking.

"I should be afraid she'd put cold poison in my tea," said Tom.

"O Tom!" cried Katie; "you do say such wicked things."

"Better that than *do* them," answered Tom. "That's what Miriam would like to do. She'd see me with the plague to-morrow, if she could."

Katie shook her head. "She doesn't mean one-half of what she says."

"She's a nasty, disagreeable thing," said Tom.

"I wish she'd had a brother," said Katie, thoughtfully. "It must be very bad to be without."

"I'm glad I'm yours instead of hers," said Tom; "that's all!"

Mrs. Rivers always left a little feast for them if she went out—some sweet-cake and preserve; and Susan had made them some dough-nuts, of which both children were particularly fond. But Tom appeared to have no appetite. "I'm shivering all over," said he when Katie remarked on it.

"Oh, Tom!" cried she; "in August! After that walk through the sun, too. Eat some more. You know papa says food is like fuel to the engine fire."

But Tom shook his head, and pushed away his plate with the unfinished dough-nut on it.

"The sight of it makes one feel bad," said he. So Katie ate no more; and very soon they left the table and went out of doors. Mrs. Rivers had given permission for them to wait up till her return, which might be rather late, as she intended going all the way to Bermondsey; but Tom grew tired of sitting up as soon as dusk came on. He felt so drowsy, and his head began to ache.

"You'd better take some rhubarb, hadn't you?" suggested Katie, who knew her mother's remedies, and never stopped to think about a nasty dose. But Tom shuddered and shook his head, and said that he should go to bed; so Katie went up too.

Tom slept very heavily that night, and when Katie roused him next morning he drowsed off again. It was rather early, for it was Susan's day out, and Katie had promised her some flowers to take home. Susan lived in London, and her parents always looked for the lovely nosegays she brought home. "The flowers make us young again," they said. Katie called to Tom as she went down; but still he did not rouse. A weight was on his head, and all his limbs seemed made of lead. Katie cut the flowers, and put them in the cool in water; then she went underneath Tom's window, and gently threw little bits of gravel up against the glass, in hopes of attracting his attention. She wished that he would come, for after the flowers she had given Tab and Zillah on the previous afternoon, she had to strip her garden-bed to get a bunch for Susan; and then it wasn't half so nice as usual. But Tom drowsed on until the bell rung for prayers, and still he didn't come downstairs. "Tom can't be well," said Mrs. Rivers, looking puzzled; and she at once went to his room.

She came down with a serious face, to mix a dose for him. "Tom doesn't seem at all the thing," said she.

Susan was waiting near the door to take her place for prayers. "I'd better not go out to-day, ma'am, perhaps," said she. "If Master Tom is going to be ill, you might be glad of me."

But Mrs. Rivers would not hear of disappointing her. "You're a good girl, Susan," answered she; "but your mother is expecting you. She would think that something was the matter if you did not come. Besides," she added hopefully, "it is nothing serious. Master Tom was walking in the sun a good while yesterday. Perhaps that was the cause. This dose will set it all to rights."

Susan "hoped it might;" and her mistress went upstairs to administer the potion.

Directly prayers were over, Susan bustled about to put things straight; then quickly changed her working-dress, and hurried down, Katie meeting her at the foot of the staircase with the nosegay carefully wrapped round in damp moss and waterproofed tea-paper to keep it fresh. Half-an-hour later Susan was well on her way, with a happy smile upon her face as she thought of her mother hurrying to the station to welcome her. Meanwhile

Katie was to be her mother's right hand for the day; so she went into the kitchen to see what she could do. But Mrs. Rivers had gone up to see to Tom, who seemed getting worse.

"Doctors always say that sickness is one of nature's remedies," said she to Mr. Rivers, who was starting off to business. "I shall let it take its course a bit, and see how Tom gets on." So Katie, finding that her mother did not come, drew water from the boiler to wash up the breakfast things. It was the first time she had attempted such a thing; but Katie was a handy girl, and not above a servant's work because her mother was a lady. She had just finished when Mrs. Rivers came down.

"Tom is asleep now," said she. "I hope he will be better when he wakes, or I shall wish that Susan hadn't gone."

"Oh, but think how disappointed she would have been!" cried Katie. "And there really isn't much to do. I can answer the door bell whilst you're upstairs with Tom."

"There's dinner to think about," said Mrs. Rivers. "One thing, there is cold meat—"

"And the potatoes are already scraped," said Katie, thoughtful as a woman; "I saw them in the bowl. And let me make the pie, mamma. Oh, do! perhaps poor Tom would eat a bit if he knew that it was mine."

Mrs. Rivers had intended only to put a simple milk-pudding in the oven, as she always did on Susan's holidays; but finding Katie so anxious to make a trial of her skill, she gave permission; so with the article on pastry-making open before her, Katie set to work, rolling out her crust most carefully, and marking it in scallops round the edge. Very well it turned out, too, when at length dinnertime arrived. Mrs. Rivers praised it as much as it deserved—which was saying a great deal, especially considering Katie's age and inexperience; but Tom touched not a bit. His head was splitting, and he was weary and exhausted with the sickness and the pain. He could scarcely bear the light, nor raise his heavy eyelids; yet sleep seemed to have deserted them. He lay there moaning and tossing, hot and shivering alternately.

Mrs. Rivers was becoming more and more alarmed. She took her needlework and sat up in his room, leaving Katie to pack away the dinner things in the scullery; and so the afternoon wore on. At length she went downstairs again to Katie, who was just about to lay the cloth for tea.

"I think Tom ought to have a doctor, Katie dear," said she. "I'm afraid that he is going to be seriously ill."

CHAPTER XIX.

KATIE'S FEAR.

KATIE looked up with a very frightened face. Miriam's words about the plague flashed through her head. "I hope that Tom and Katie Rivers may be the first to catch it," Miriam had said.

"You had better run and see if Digby has gone home," Mrs. Rivers went on. "If not, send him up to Dr. Furnace's at once. I wish that your papa were here. But he is stock-taking, you see, and will be late again to-night."

Katie ran away with the message, calling Digby as she went; but she searched the premises in vain. The man had already gone home to his tea.

"And won't be back until it's time to put the pony to, to fetch your papa from the station," said Mrs. Rivers. "I wish that Susan had not gone to-day."

"Let me run for Dr. Furnace," said Katie eagerly. "It's such a long way for you by yourself," objected her mamma; "and dusk comes on so quickly these late summer evenings."

"I'll run every step of the way, mamma," urged Katie. "*Do* let me go! It may be too late if we delay."

Mrs. Rivers smiled, in spite of her own fears. "Tom isn't quite so bad as that, I hope," she answered reassuringly. "Still, I would rather Dr. Furnace saw him before morning; he seems so feverish."

"Then *do* let me go," begged Katie. "I promise you I'll run."

So Mrs. Rivers gave consent. "Only there's no necessity to run," said she. But anxiety lent wings to Katie's feet, and she sped swiftly along the lane and up by the plantation, where the birds, too busy over family considerations all day long, were gossiping among the boughs.

Katie did not hear them, for Miriam's words were in her ears; she had not even time to stop and reason, or she would have recognized how ridiculous it was to think that God would let her schoolfellow's wish work mischief against Tom. But Katie thought of nothing but Tom's danger. A blackbird even flew across the road, not half-a-dozen yards ahead, with a startled "Quivit! quick! quick! quick!" But she hardly noticed it. Her mind was full of that one thought.

Miriam was inside the garden gate with Madge, as she ran by, and stared to see her flying past at such a rate. " Have you lost anything? " she called out in a jeering tone. " ' K. K.—careless Katie.' Have it cried."

" ' Oh yes; lost my wits' ! " added Madge, raising her voice in imitation of the old town-crier. But Katie did not heed. On she sped, past the farm-yard gate, past the church, and down the hill, panting and breathless, without a respite, till the steep ascent up the other side forced her to slacken pace.

Mrs. Bull was in the honeysuckle porch as Katie came in sight, toiling up the road. She stepped outside, and leisurely came down the path to meet her. " Did they get home safe, miss, our two little gals ? " asked she when Katie got quite close. But Katie's panting breath and hot, flushed face told plainly that something was the matter.

" Who's been frightening you, missie ? " she asked before Katie had time to answer her other question. " Come inside a bit."

But Katie shook her head. " I've been running, Mrs. Bull; that's all," cried she. " Tom's ill, and Susan's out; I'm fetching Dr. Furnace in a hurry."

" Bless the dear young lady, what a heat you're in ! " cried Mrs. Bull; " you'll do yourself a mischief running so. Now you come in and rest, and Dick shall run for you."

But Katie would not rest until her message was delivered; and on she went, resuming her quick pace so soon as ever she had gained the brow of the hill. Five minutes later she had rung the surgery bell, and was waiting breathlessly, with throbbing pulses and trembling limbs, to know if Dr. Furnace was at home. Luckily he was. "How fortunate you came just now!" said he. "There's nothing like being in good time with the physic. I've only just come in, so the horse is still in the shafts. Sit down and rest a minute, whilst I take a cup of tea, and we'll ride back together."

CHAPTER XX.

SUSAN GIVES GOOD ADVICE.

POOR Tom had typhoid fever. For a fortnight Dr. Furnace came to see him twice a day, and there was terrible anxiety throughout the house. Mrs. Rivers was in his sick-room night and day, and Katie had to shift as best she could, making her papa's tea of a morning, sitting down alone to her solitary dinner, and going to bed in the dusk without her mother's good-night kiss. No wonder she was miserable. She had not seen Tom since he was taken bad, and she often cried herself to sleep, thinking how he might never speak to her again.

Susan found her so, one night, lying with her face buried in the pillow, sobbing as if her heart would break. Now Susan was a simple-hearted, Christian girl. "Miss Katie, darling, don't take on like that," said she. "Master Tom'll get well yet, please God."

But Katie still sobbed on. "It's all that wicked Miriam," cried she. "I hate her, that I do."

"Why Miss Miriam?" asked Susan in surprise.

"What can Miss Miriam have to do with Master Tom's falling ill?"

"She said she hoped he would," sobbed Katie; and by degrees she got the whole history out, between her sobs, of what Miriam and Madge had said about the plague.

"You silly goose!" said Susan, coaxingly, near crying too, for sympathy, to tell the truth. "He's got typhoid fever, not the plague."

"She didn't mean the *plague*, I don't suppose," sobbed Katie. "She didn't much care what he had, so long as he was bad."

"And if she did," rejoined the maid, "what difference would it make, I'd like to know? Fevers don't depend upon ill-natured children's whims and wishes, I should hope. Now just stop crying, and dry your eyes and think."

Katie checked her sobs immediately, half ashamed. "What made the fever come, then?" asked she in a tearful voice, trying to look up.

Susan sat down on the bed. It was very late, and she was tired, for illness makes a deal of work. "You see, I don't know very much," said she, "because I don't read many books. Your papa could tell you better; but I *know* it wasn't anything to do with what Miss Miriam wished."

"She was nasty about our having Tab and Zillah down, you know," explained Katie, trying to steady her voice; "because Tom made her angry teasing her, and so she wouldn't help. She never speaks to either of us now."

"Very silly and unchristian, too," said Susan, smothering a yawn. "You see," she went on presently, "as to how and why fevers come. I don't think God would be unfair enough—if that's a word I may use with proper reverence about Almighty God—to put 'em in the hands of spiteful people, just like weapons to do harm with. I shouldn't love God if I thought he'd do like that; should you, Miss Katie dear?"

Katie answered "No," and sobbed a little more.

"Do you think Tab and Zillah could have brought the fever down?" she asked by-and-by, sitting up in bed. "The slum they live in is a nasty, dirty place, you know," she added, just a trifle doubtfully.

But Susan shook her head. "The fever Master Tom's got ain't like scarlatina," answered she. "Nurse was telling me so yesterday. She says that it comes from drinking bad water, and from nasty smells, and that people don't catch it from each other's clothes, but because they smell the same bad smells, and get their drinking water from the self-same pump. That's why I've got such particular orders as to all the drinking water being boiled. It's to be hoped no more of us will take it, too."

"And Tab and Zillah," added Katie, thinking what a sad end to their holiday. "Poor Tab and Zillah couldn't have such nursing as Tom has."

"But God takes care of the poor," said Susan trustfully. "He wouldn't let 'em have a holiday to go back ill."

"And now I'm off to bed," said Susan presently; "and mind you go to sleep. Your pillow is sopped," she added, turning dry side upward, and laying the bedclothes straight. "Now when I'm gone, if I were you I'd get out of bed and say my prayers again; and then I'd go right off to sleep, and leave the rest to God. Depend upon it, he knows better what's the best for Master Tom than you or I."

Next morning Tom was pronounced out of danger. The crisis had passed during the night, and the doctor said that all would now be well. Katie had to run away to hide her tears of joy when first she heard the news, but Susan took no pains to hide her own. "I said—please God—that he'd get well," said she; "and, Miss Katie, I asked again about the way the fever comes. I asked the doctor this time; so it must be right. He says it's something wrong about the drains; and when Master Tom is strong enough, we're all to go away and have 'em set to rights. So Tab and Zillah ain't to blame; nor yet Miss Miriam—only for the will, not for the deed."

CHAPTER XXI.

MIRIAM'S EYES ARE OPENED.

THAT morning was the first day of the autumn term at school. Katie set out with a light heart. She had seen Tom, and though terribly shocked at his wasted appearance, she knew that he was safe, as he had smiled at her.

She sang for joy as she ran down the drive; and all the birds seemed singing too—the robins in particular, for it was now the middle of September.

Miriam was on in front, but guessing who was following her, she took care not to turn her head. But Katie was far too happy to feel annoyed. Miriam had changed her shoes and got into her place when Katie walked up the schoolroom to speak to Miss Ansell.

"'K. K.—careless Katie,'" whispered Madge, loud enough for all the girls to hear.

"She's going to be put down, I'll be bound," said Miriam, as Katie, after standing by the desk in conversation with Miss Ansell several minutes, turned back to take her place. Her eyes were moist and her face flushed, for she could not tell her good news about Tom without a little cry. Now Miriam had been away a week or two, and did not know about the danger Tom had been in; and seeing Katie's troubled look, concluded it was due to something Miss Ansell had said. But Miriam proved wrong, for Katie was moved up instead of down, and school commenced.

Miriam did so much whispering and tittering that morning that she was kept behind, and even Madge went off without her. When at last she came out to the cloak-room for her hat, she found Katie still there. "I thought I'd wait for you, Miriam," said she. "It's so dull to go home all alone."

"You're very kind, K. K.," said Miriam sarcastically; "but I'm sure you need not have troubled."

Miriam was fumbling at her shoes, trying hard to do the buttons up with her fingers.

"You've left your hook at home!" cried Katie, pulling one out of her pocket. "Use mine."

But Miriam shook her head. "No, thank you, Kate," said she, getting up to reach her hat, with only half the buttons done. "I never borrow other people's property."

Katie tried again, determined to make peace, if possible. It seemed so terrible to think how the "sun" of poor Tom's life had nearly "set upon their wrath;" and in her joy and thankfulness for his recovery she was ready to do anything to win Miriam back. "Won't you be friends with me to-day, Miriam?" said she, stooping to pick up a glove which Miriam had dropped.

"I'm in a hurry," answered Miriam, snatching at the glove without a word of thanks, and pushing past her to the door.

"I've waited on purpose, so that I might walk with you," said Katie coaxingly. "I want to tell you something."

"It'll keep till some other time, I'll be bound," said Miriam carelessly, still pushing on. "Some people's secrets aren't worth hearing. Perhaps you've got your locket back?"

"It's about Tom," said Katie, hurrying after her.

"He's been punished long enough, I suppose," said Miriam. "Is he sorry yet?"

"I don't know," answered Katie. "He *was* wrong at the first, of course; I told him so. But I wanted you to know how ill he has been. He nearly died last night. Miriam! don't you care?" and Katie's voice trembled so that even Miriam, in her heart of hearts, was softened. But pride still whispered, "What do you care if he *has* been ill, or nearly died? What is he to you? He has offended you; and you don't care a pin for him."

"What's that to me!" cried she aloud.

"O Miriam!" cried Katie; "don't you *really*

care? You didn't surely *mean* it when you said you wished he'd catch the plague? Do let me come and walk with you."

Miriam still hurried on; but conscience smote her. She remembered her own words quite well—" What if Tom had really died!" Still pride whispered, " Don't let Katie see you're sorry." " Tom's a nasty, disagreeable boy," said she. " I hate you both."

" Tom teased you *once*," said Katie, hurrying after her. " But I think if you were ill, instead of him, he would be ready to forgive you and be friends."

Uncle Merry's words came back to Miriam. " Now when I'm gone," her great-uncle had said, " just think what you can do to show Tom that you're ready to be friends." And that, in turn, brought back to mind how generously Tom had risked himself to save her from the adder. But for Tom she might have been a cripple now; or worse still, cold and stiff beneath the cold, dark earth out in the churchyard yonder. Miriam shuddered. Somehow she could not think about the brighter side of death just then. She knew she had been wrong; and only those who copy Christ can feel that death is passing into life.

" He wouldn't like to have been teased himself," said she. " It isn't nice." But she slackened pace;

and Katie, with one bound, was at her side, and slipped a hand into her arm.

"Do let's be friends again," she begged. "I think if you would come half-way, and let Tom see you wanted to, he'd make it up, and say that he's most sorry."

"All very fine!" grumbled Miriam, "when he's most in the wrong." That word "most" slipped out unawares. Miriam did not mean to admit that she was in the wrong at all; but her better nature took her off her guard, and spoke the truth.

"Tom *was* wrong first," said Katie; "but then you never thanked him when he sprained his foot in saving you. And you don't know how much he suffered."

Miriam had not cared a bit about it at the time. Her mother had spoken seriously of her ingratitude, but all to no effect; and since she had almost forgotten about it. But now she seemed to see it in a different light, and she was sorry all at once.

"Poor Tom!" said she, quite gently. "All for me! Poor Tom!"

That afternoon Miriam started earlier than usual for school, in order that she might run up the lane to Katie's first, to call for her; and in her hand she took two lovely tea-rosebuds, the pride and glory of her bush.

"These are for Tom," said she.

CHAPTER XXII.

TOM'S GOOD FAIRY.

THE two girls were firm friends after this; and every morning Miriam ran down the lane to take a nosegay of fresh flowers for Tom.

At present Tom was far too weak to notice much; but Miriam was content that they should stand by his bedside, so that when he came to ask who gathered them he might know she wanted to make friends. At length, one morning, when he was getting better, Katie went upstairs, as usual, with Miriam's flowers. Tom was propped up on his pillows, taking some beef-tea. It was the first time he had been able to hold the cup to his own lips. His eyes brightened as Katie entered.

"They *are* nice," said he, in his poor, weak voice.

"I'm glad you like them," answered Katie, cheerfully, with a meaning glance up in her mother's face.

"They smell so sweet," said Tom; "and it's so nice to have fresh ones every day. I'm so tired of all the things in this old room."

"I didn't know you noticed anything," said Katie, looking down affectionately at his thin, pale face. "It shows you're getting better fast."

Tom was certainly much better, and making good progress. He had not tried to talk of anything till then, but had only just lain still and taken what they gave him with a smile. But now it seemed as if he had roused to life again. "Roses, too," said he. "Where did you get those orange-coloured ones? We haven't any like them in the garden."

"Miriam brought them for you," answered Katie.

"Miriam?" echoed Tom.

"Yes," said Mrs. Rivers, coming to the bedside for the empty cup. "It is Miriam who has brought the flowers every day. But you see we were so quiet about the name of your good fairy, that you never suspected who she was."

Tom's eyes filled with tears. He was still so weak that the news was almost more than he could bear. His mother feared it was exciting him too much.

"You will soon be strong enough to thank her for yourself," said she. "But Katie must not keep her waiting any longer now, or they will both be late for school." So Katie said good-bye, and ran downstairs.

As soon as she was gone Mrs. Rivers re-arranged

the pillows, so that Tom could lie down; and Tom shut his eyes, and lay so still that his mother thought he was asleep, and went downstairs. But Tom was not asleep. He was only tired with the effort he had made; and as he lay he was thinking about Miriam. She wanted to be friends; he was quite sure of that, and he could not but be glad. And yet just one thing troubled him. If Miriam made up the quarrel while he lay there quite incapable of teasing her or doing any harm, would it not make him look rather small? Tom wanted it made up, but pride was in the way. He had risked his life to save her from the adder all to no purpose; and now that he was weak and ill, he did not choose to be forgiven for the *little* wrong that he had done her in the spring-time long ago. Had he stopped to think, he would have recognized that forgiveness, in itself, is far more noble than any show of greatness such as pride would prompt him to maintain; because, to be like Christ is the greatest thing that any one can do. And Christ forgave his enemies.

Katie went and sat a long while by Tom's bedside that evening. Now that he was fairly convalescent, she might talk to him; and though Tom was not strong enough at present to talk much, it amused him to listen to all she had to chat about.

That very morning, as it chanced, too, she had

seen a squirrel in the plantation. "He ran up the very tree where you cut your initials," said she.

"That was in the Easter holidays," said Tom; "and now it's autumn. What a time it seems since I went out!"

"And what a lot you've grown these last six weeks!" added Katie. "People always do in fevers; so I've heard."

Tom lay still awhile. "Katie!" said he presently.

Katie looked up from her work.

"I almost wish that Miriam hadn't brought me flowers every day."

"Why, Tom?" asked Katie, in surprise. "I thought you'd be so pleased."

"Only," reasoned Tom, "it makes me look so small, just as if she pitied me, now I'm so ill."

"I don't think that matters one single bit," said Katie.

"You see," continued Tom, "I *was* in the wrong a little bit at first. I oughtn't to have teased her when I saw she took it so; but she was horribly ungrateful afterwards, and it doesn't look very nice for her to come and *forgive* me when I can't move hand or foot. It makes me look so *small*," repeated Tom.

"You mean that you would rather have gone to *her*, and asked her to forgive you whilst you were quite strong, and able to go on teasing if you chose," said Katie.

But Tom shook his head. "I couldn't go so far as *that*," said he. "That would be humbling myself a little *too* much. It isn't even as if she were a boy."

Tom's pride was far from conquered yet.

Katie cast about to think what she could say to change his mind. "We ought not to be proud, Tom," said she. "Papa read at prayers this very morning how God resists the proud; and Christ forgave his enemies. You would really be the greatest that way, after all."

Tom lay still, and said no more.

"Mamma was saying," Katie went on, by-and-by, "that if you are as much better to-morrow as she expects, you may perhaps get up a little while. Then Miriam might come and give you the flowers herself. May she?" Katie added timidly.

Tom hesitated half a minute; then he answered, "If she likes; but mind, I've no intention of begging her pardon, or doing anything of that sort."

Poor Tom! how sad to have such a mountain of pride to overcome.

Next morning, however, Miriam did not come as usual. The sky was rather threatening, and Katie accounted for the fact in that way, thinking that she had been anxious to get to school before the wet came on. But Miriam was not in her place at school; and when Katie went to see what was amiss, she found her lying on the sofa, feeling very ill.

"I'm glad that it's half-holiday," said she. "To-morrow I shall be all right, no doubt; and I shall have a lovely rose for Tom."

"Mamma says you may give it him yourself to-morrow afternoon," said Katie, as she bade good-bye.

But Miriam did not come, for she got worse instead of better; and by next afternoon she was seriously ill.

CHAPTER XXIII.

AS FIRE MELTS THE DROSS AWAY.

TOM went on improving very rapidly. Once he got on to the sofa he was able to get up for a little every day. Of course he tired very quickly. At first he had to be carried from his bed, and could not talk for long, nor hold a book; but all he wanted was to build up the strength the fever had consumed, and considering the quantities of good things that Tom devoured, it was not surprising that the work went on so fast. At length the doctor said he might go out a little in the middle of the day.

Tom was longing to be out once more, and Katie was quite ready to push the old chair round the garden paths, and up and down the lane. But just as this permission came the weather closed in wet.

Meanwhile Miriam had been worse than even Tom. The same infection which had poisoned Mr. Rivers's well had poisoned Mr. Grayson's too. For many days poor Miriam had lain in the very jaws of death. At length one night, however, her delirium subsided, and she sank into a sleep so still and death-like that parents, nurse, and doctor watched by her with bated breath. All through the night and all next day they watched her, whilst the rain beat mournfully against the window pane, as if the skies were sorrowing for their grief. More than once the doctor held a mirror to her lips, to see if she still breathed; and more than once he feared the heart had ceased to beat. But at last, when evening came, just as the rain ceased, and the setting sun broke out, her eyelids opened, and she drew a long, deep breath, then fell into a sweet, refreshing sleep. And they thanked God, knowing she was saved.

Katie was sitting near the window in Tom's room, learning a lesson, when the cloud lifted. "You will be able to go out to-morrow, Tom," said she, looking up from her book; and she went on planning all that they would do, until it grew dark, and Mrs. Rivers came up with a light to help Tom into bed.

She had not long left him, with the bell-rope handy on his pillow, in case he wanted anything, when Katie came upstairs again and crept into the room tiptoe.

"Are you awake, Tom?" whispered she.

Tom answered "Yes," and moved his head up on the pillow, wondering what she could want.

"I came to tell you, Tom," said Katie, "Susan has been to inquire how Miriam is. She's safe, Tom. Oh! I am so glad; aren't you? She'll get well now."

To Katie's infinite surprise, Tom hid his face in his pillow for a minute, then burst out crying. He too had been near death, and knew the utter helplessness of being very weak. And he was so thankful Miriam had not died before he had a chance of making up their quarrel. Katie laid her cheek against his hair, and cried some tears of gladness too, and by-and-by Tom raised his head again.

"Now I know God answers prayer," said he, when he could find his voice, " because he's answered mine."

"And mine," his sister answered softly, with her arm still round his neck.

Ah! Tom had learned to pray, *not* on his knees, since he had been too weak to kneel, and very different prayers from those he used to gabble over, night and morning, when he was in health. God teaches us by suffering sometimes, as the fire melts the dross away and makes the metal pure.

CHAPTER XXIV.

THE NEW SCHEME.

THE girls at school had been terribly shocked at the news of Miriam's illness, but now that she was safely on the road to convalescence, they laughed and chattered merrily once more, as school-girls do. Only Madge seemed dull and wretched still. She came and went alone, and no one seemed to care for her.

Katie mentioned it to Miriam, one day when she went to sit with her.

"It seems too bad by half," said Katie, as they talked. "It isn't Christian to treat her so; and yet it's her own fault, as much as any one's."

"I'm most to blame," said Miriam penitently. "I made her wild against you—her and Terry Grainger—and then the girls took up your side, and made us worse than ever. But she never would have quarrelled with you if it hadn't been for me." So Miriam had her punishment to bear, like all who cherish evil tempers; and thus the weeks went on.

Meanwhile another scheme was being set on foot.

It was first canvassed in Mrs. Grayson's sitting-room, where Miriam, still very weak, was lying on the couch. "The girls all want to know what we can do for charity this Christmas-time," said Katie, coming in one afternoon, as she so often did, upon her way from school. "Can you suggest?"

"A Christmas dinner," answered Miriam promptly. "Nice roast-beef and hot plum-pudding for a hundred children. Could we manage it?"

Katie didn't know. "The girls all want to do something for Tab and Zillah Wimbly, who were here last summer," said she. "We've got an interest in them, you see."

Miriam saw the force of Katie's argument at once. "And I may help this time?" said she.

"Of course," answered Katie, giving her hand a squeeze. "I wonder what we could collect?"

"A lot," said Miriam, "if everybody gave up Christmas-trees. And who wants Christmas-trees when there are children starving? I wish I hadn't bought that stupid locket with the money Uncle Merry gave me," she went on presently.

"Lockets aren't of much use, after all," said Katie, sighing, with a thought of her sad accident. "I've been just as happy without mine—that is, I should have been if I had never had it to lose."

Mrs. Grayson came in just then, and heard what they were talking about. "I know what I should recommend," said she. "If you children can collect enough, why not purchase a stocking-knitter for Tab and Zillah, and so put them in the way of earning money for themselves?"

So the girls were taken into council, and a price-list was obtained, and the stocking-knitter found to be within their reach. "Whatever else we get beyond the price of it," they all agreed, "shall go towards some Christmas-dinner fund."

CHAPTER XXV.

UNCLE MERRY'S BAND.

MIRIAM'S recovery was very slow and tedious. She had been much worse than Tom, and her strength was longer coming back. But she had little chance of being dull, the girls were all so kind. Madge Tewson was the only one who did not come.

"I can't think *why* she has deserted me," Miriam often said to Katie. "We've been such friends—especially since I quarrelled with you and Tom."

"Perhaps she's vexed you made it up with us," suggested Katie.

"Or thinks that I don't want her now," said Miriam; and she tried to send her messages by Katie and the other girls. But Madge took care that none of them should have a chance of giving messages. She kept all to herself, and never spoke to any one if she could help. Poor Madge was very wretched, if they had but known the truth.

About the middle of November, Great-uncle Merry came to see how Miriam was getting on.

"There's room for Tom and Katie's 'fresh-air mission' here," said he, on finding she was strong enough to be moved.

"O Uncle Merry!" Miriam laughed. "As if *I* had need of charity."

"Of course you have," replied her uncle cheerily. "We all have need of charity; for 'charity' is *love*, you know,—not always *giving alms*, but just the love that goes about this earth, endeavouring to make the crooked places straight, and drive away the clouds, and scatter seeds of kindness 'for our reaping by-and-by.'

"You see," continued Uncle Merry, "there are heaps of people haven't got the smallest coin to spare to do a deed of what commonly goes by the name of 'charity.' But they can give kind words and gentle deeds, if they have loving hearts inside their breasts, and be no whit the poorer for it all the while. Now I know fifty little children near my home who go about in this way doing charity. They pick up little toddlers who have tumbled down, and wipe away their tears; they dance the baby when he's fretful with a tooth and mother's arms are tired out with nursing him. They warm their father's slippers when he comes home cold from work. They leave off in the middle of a game to help an old man's load up on his back. They return soft answers in place of crabby, sour ones, and give their teachers just as little trouble as they can. They do more good, and make more sunshine in their little world, without a penny of their own, than many grown-up people do with all the gold and silver they possess."

"What children are they, Uncle Merry?" asked Miriam.

"Just little boys and girls, six, eight, ten, twelve, who live in courts and alleys near my home," Great-uncle Merry answered. "Poor people's children, mostly, too. Their fathers are bricklayers, painters, porters, carpenters, day-labourers, who get what work they can, and sometimes none at all. Their mothers wash, and scrub, and sew, to help pay rent and firing and food. Some have sick fathers or mothers; some have none at all. Some few are comfortably off, and one or two are almost rich, but they are thought no more of than the rest. They all are simply 'Band of Kindness' children—pledged to do whatever little acts of love and help they can to all with whom they have to do."

"Was that what you were thinking of that day when I told you about Tom Rivers, Uncle Merry?" asked Miriam. "You said that you would like to see us 'Band of Kindness' children."

"Quite right," replied her uncle. "I recollect

quite well. It came into my head that many of my hard-worked, ill-fed little friends would put you two to shame, with your many great advantages, and your disagreeable tempers."

"O Uncle Merry!" cried Miriam, with tears starting to her eyes, "we have made it all up now."

"And right glad I am to hear it," returned Uncle Merry heartily. "I hope you won't *un*make it again by any accident; and as I'm a member of the Band of Kindness too, I won't say any more *un*kind things about it."

"Uncle Merry!" said Miriam suddenly, "could we have a Band of Kindness here?"

"Why not?" asked Uncle Merry. "Wherever there are children there can be a 'band.' For band means 'union,' you know. It means that you all join together and try to keep before each others minds the loveliness and happiness of doing good. *My* little children meet each Sunday morning whilst the big folks are at church, and tell each other what they have been doing all the week. Sometimes they have sad tales to tell, of how the bad part of them got the upper hand and made them selfish and *un*kind; but they like to tell each other, so they say, because it makes them feel ashamed, and then they try so much the harder all next week."

"But we're all comfortably off," said Miriam.

"We don't have things to make us wicked and bad-tempered, like your poor children do."

"That's very true," returned her uncle; "so you ought to have fewer tales of failure to relate. But perhaps that's just the very snare wherein your danger lies. You know, it's just when people think themselves the most secure that they're most off their guard. Remember that! But don't you recollect that text about 'making a great feast'? 'Call the poor, the maimed, the halt, the blind,' Christ said. And I should like to say the same about your 'band.' Don't keep it to yourselves. Get poor children to join. You know many 'halt, and maimed, and blind;' some whose tempers trip them up at every step; some whose hands have never learned to serve the Master by these gentle little deeds of every day that make life sweet; some whose eyes want opening to the great reward that comes to all who seek not their own but others' happiness. Get *them* to join your band."

CHAPTER XXVI.

WON OVER.

A WEEK later Miriam and her mamma accompanied Great-uncle Merry to the sea. "What *will* your 'Band of Kindness' children do without you, Uncle Merry?" Miriam said, flying across the country in the train.

"They know a certain little sick girl needs my kindness just now," replied her uncle, "so they're 'kind' enough to do without me for a little while. They are very fond of me, but they are not selfish, don't you see, because they're 'Band of Kindness' children."

"Fond of you! I should think they are, you dear old Uncle Merry!" Miriam exclaimed.

Miriam was obliged to have a chair at first, because she could not walk; but very soon the sea-air made her ravenous,—and when the appetite returns, strength very quickly follows. In a fortnight's time she was almost as well as she had ever been—only, like Tom, very tall and thin.

Meanwhile, Tom and Katie worked away for the "Band of Kindness" with a right good-will. A number of the boys and girls from both their schools enrolled their names at once; and each one undertook to bring some other to the opening meeting, when Miriam's Uncle Merry had promised to be there, to give them a fair start and draw up the rules.

Tom undertook to ask Dick Bull.

"You fought him once, to teach him to be kind to Tim," said Katie. "But I fancy Tab did far more by her gentleness. He hasn't teased him half so much since she was here, so Mrs. Bull was telling me the other day."

Then Katie had to choose whom she would ask; being one of those brave people who never shun hard tasks, she chose Madge. "I'll keep on trying till I win her over," Katie said.

The first thing was to get the chance. A long while Katie watched in vain for it; but all comes in good time to those who wait. One very gusty, rainy morning, Katie, coming home from school, caught sight of Madge ahead. She quickened pace, in hopes of catching up with her; but Madge was hurrying, so that Katie almost had to run to gain upon her ever such a little.

It was blowing quite a "capful," as the sailors say, which made it difficult to push along so fast. Every now and then she had to stop and let the gusts go by; and once or twice her umbrella narrowly escaped turning inside out. But then, of course, Madge had the same difficulties to contend against, so that the odds were pretty fair. At length, however, her footsteps reached Madge's ear, and she looked round to see who might be following her.

Now Madge was at a sharp bend in the road, and she forgot that when she turned the corner the wind would blow the other way. Just when she was completely off her guard the gust tore up, with all the mischief that a gust can boast, rushed under her umbrella, till all the spokes bent backward like reeds before the flood, and seizing on her hat, in less than no time had it whisked from off her head, and capering along towards Katie through the puddles. At the same instant the strap she carried in her other hand gave way, and all her books went tumbling in the mud.

Such a picture of vexation and dismay it is difficult to conceive: the wrecked umbrella utterly refusing to come down; the hat escaping like a mad thing from a cage; poor Madge—her hair all streaming in the wind and wet—completely stupified, not knowing where to turn or what to do.

Katie dodged the hat, and caught it cleverly; but it was too bedrabbled for any head to wear. "What *will* you do?" cried she, now joining Madge. " Come under my umbrella. You *must*," she cried, as Madge refused. "Pick up the books; there's room for some of them in my satchel. Oh! never mind the mud. Mine are all covered; so it won't soil them." And chattering on good-naturedly, she soon had half of them put up.

"You must carry these," she added—"so. Now take my arm, and keep as close against me as you can, and we shall get along quite well."

Madge scarcely spoke a word the whole way home, and that afternoon she did not go to school. Her mother thought that one such wetting was enough in one short day; besides, she had no hat except her Sunday one. But next morning Katie found Madge waiting in the cloak-room for her.

"I've covered all your books for you," said Katie, as she put her satchel down; "they were hardly soiled inside. How's your hat?"

But Madge, instead of answering, held out a little packet towards her. "I never meant to be so wicked," she stammered out; "indeed, indeed I didn't! I found it on the road near Mrs. Bull's, and thought I'd keep it back a little, just to tease. I thought it would be fun. But afterwards I got ashamed, and the longer I delayed the worse it was; and—there it is; and please forgive me, Katie, and get them all to let me join the 'band.'"

Katie gave a cry of glad surprise. It was her lost locket, safe and sound. And Madge was won.

CHAPTER XXVII.

A MERRY CHRISTMAS.

CHRISTMAS-EVE had come, and it was nearly dark. The night before, an inch or two of snow had fallen; but it lay only upon the roofs and round the ledges of the chimney-pots. In the roadways and on the pavements traffic and foot-passengers had worn it into cold, wet slush. At dusk, however, the clouds rolled back, a crust formed on the slush, and there was every prospect of a bitter night.

Tab was looking out across the whitened tiles, when Zillah climbed the stairs. There was a gleam of firelight in the room—a luxury not always to be met with in a garret such as theirs; but Tab had turned away from that. She was thinking of the Christmas-eve before, when there was not a bit of fire in the grate, and nothing but dry bread to eat —nor much of that. Tab's was a grateful soul.

Zillah burst in, full of life. "My! the shops are *splendid*, Tab," cried she. "Such a flare of gas, and beef and geese and turkeys all made fine with coloured ribbons—blue and red. You can warm your hands there while you look. And dolls, and toys, and—" Zillah ran on with a list of all the wonders she had seen. "My feet ain't cold a bit to-night," she added, glancing at her slushy boots, "although it is so dirty underfoot."

Tab glanced down at the boots, which were stout and strong. "Lots of other people's are, to-night," said she. "God's very good to us, Zill, ain't he?"

Zillah didn't answer this remark. "I saw some lovely pudding in a window," she ran on—"all plums, and steaming hot. Tab, shouldn't you just like a slice?"

"P'raps father'll bring some, if he's lucky getting jobs," said Tab.

"Most people have got something good to-night," said Zillah, hooking up her jacket on a nail behind the door. "They'll go out with their baskets presently, and spend."

"Not all," said Tab. "We hadn't anything to spend last year. Some haven't this year, either."

Just as Tab said these words a sound of footsteps on the stairs attracted their attention. "There's dad," cried Zillah eagerly, running to the door. Perhaps Tab had asked him to buy some pudding for a treat. Zill's mouth had watered when she saw it steaming there behind the glass.

A MERRY CHRISTMAS. 155

Tab went to get the candle down; but Zillah uttered an astonished cry. It was not her father's footsteps they had heard. Cautiously feeling his way up in the dim light of the staircase was a man whom Zillah did not know. He had a deal box on his shoulder, and a hamper in one hand.

"Tab and Zillah Wimbly?" asked he, stopping at the door; then, as Zillah nodded, he came right in and set his load down on the floor. "And a merry Christmas to you wi' 'em," he added, as he turned to go. "There's summat good inside, that many folks'd envy you to-night."

"Let's wait till father comes, to open 'em," was Tab's idea; but Zillah's fingers couldn't wait. She was already on her knees, and pulling at the knots.

Zillah clapped her hands, and Tab's eyes filled with tears, at sight of all the things they found inside. Tea and sugar, butter, oatmeal, bacon, cheese; a Christmas pudding, raisins, figs, nuts, oranges; and on the top a lovely Christmas card.

"What's in the box?" cried Zillah next. But that was fastened up with nails instead of string. They tried to force it open with a fork; but the nails were in too deep. Tab got the little iron bar that served as poker; but that was twice too thick to go into the crack.

Just then a gentle rap came at the door. There stood a white-headed old gentleman, who looked as if the snow had settled on his beard and hair; but yet his face was cheery as the summer sky as he stepped in.

"A merry Christmas to you both, my dears," said he. "I see you've got your packages all right. I've come to tell you which to eat."

It was Miriam's great-uncle Merry, who had undertaken the purchase of the stocking-knitter, and followed in its train to explain its use and show them how it worked.

CHAPTER XXVIII.

"*PEACE ON EARTH, GOOD WILL TOWARD MEN.*"

CHRISTMAS morning. Miriam had looked at all her Christmas cards, and breakfasted, and fed the birds that flocked down to the kitchen door for crumbs; then, cozily wrapped up, she ran out in the cold, keen air.

Great-uncle Merry was expected by-and-by, to eat his Christmas dinner with them; but he had helped to give breakfast to some hundred little waifs and strays that morning, so he could not come until the mid-day train.

First Miriam went and looked at all her hen-house pets. She found them fluffed up like great feather balls in a sheltered nook where they could see the sun, although it failed to reach them with its feeble rays. "You'd better run about by half, you silly things!" said she, scattering them right and left. Then off she tripped to follow out her own advice, whilst the hens crept back indignant to their strip of sunshine underneath the fence.

Every splash of water in the stable-yard was frozen solid, and a fringe of white was on each jutting ledge. The frost had seized upon the damp that rose at sunset overnight, and fixed it there. It glistened in the light like powdered diamond. Every grass blade in the field was white with it; and the path, which yesterday was thick with mud, was firm and hard as a rock. Miriam ran to the plantation gate, unlatched it, and slipped through. She had not been there since her birthday picnic party ended so unhappily. But there was no fear of adders now. The dry leaves crackled under foot, the bare boughs overhead were hung with icicles like fairy stalactites, and Miriam's voice rang out among the trees for very joy of heart. For the winter sky was blue above her head, and she was well and strong again.

"Dick and Harry and Tom,"

she sang—

"Dick and Harry and Tom,
They teased the dog, and worried the cat,
And drowned the kittens in their grandfather's hat,
Did Dick and Harry and Tom."

Suddenly Miriam stopped short. She had not been thinking what she sang. The plantation had somehow put the words into her head. But as she stopped another voice took up the tune.

"Kit and Mirry and Tom,"

it sang—

"Kit and Mirry and Tom,
*They teased each other instead of the cat,
And lived by the rule of 'tit for tat,'*
Did Kit and Mirry and Tom."

And up jumped Tom Rivers, with both arms on the fence, and Katie at his side.

But Tom and Katie were not Miriam's only audience.

"Nice young people to be starting a Band of Kindness," called Uncle Merry's voice jocosely from the plantation gate.

The brave old gentleman, having caught an earlier train, had just arrived, and finding his nephew-in-law out and Mrs. Grayson busy with cook, he had come to look for Miriam to take him for a walk, to whet his appetite for dinner.

Ten minutes later Tom and Katie had been indoors with them to have some biscuits and warm milk; and the four were on the road—a happy quartet. They talked of Uncle Merry's "band," and of his waifs and strays, and heard of Tab and Zillah's great delight at all the good things they had sent, not least of all the stocking-knitter, by means of which they hoped to earn so much.

Gradually the sun rose higher in the sky, and smiled across the frost-bound earth, till icicles and frost-work all gave way before his smile. And Uncle Merry said that it was like the smile of love, that melts the frost of selfishness and scatters seeds of kindness in dark lives—the Love that came into this world that Christmas morn when angels sang their song of " peace on earth."

THE END.

www.ingramcontent.com/pod-product-compliance
Lightning Source LLC
Chambersburg PA
CBHW030307170426
43202CB00009B/910